Where do people use boats instead of cars?

Where is the longest railroad in the world?

Where was the Silk Road?

Where is Africa splitting apart?

Where do more than 17,500 islands make up a country?

Where do lemurs live?

Where is the longest fence in the world?

Where is the hadal zone?

TIME FOR KIDS

BIG BOOK OF WHERE

TIME FOR KIDS
Managing Editor, TIME FOR KIDS: Nellie Gonzalez Cutler

Book Packager: R studio T, New York City
Art Direction/Design: Raúl Rodriguez
Writer: Linda Falken
Photo Researcher: Elizabeth Vezzulla
Designer: Robert Dominguez
Fact Checkers: Ames Montgomery, Audrey Whitley

TIME HOME ENTERTAINMENT
Publisher: Jim Childs
Vice President, Brand & Digital Strategy: Steven Sandonato
Executive Director, Marketing Services: Carol Pittard
Executive Director, Retail & Special Sales: Tom Mifsud
Executive Publishing Director: Joy Butts
Director, Bookazine Development & Marketing: Laura Adam
Finance Director: Glenn Buonocore
Associate Publishing Director: Megan Pearlman
Assistant General Counsel: Helen Wan
Assistant Director, Special Sales: Ilene Schreider
Senior Book Production Manager: Susan Chodakiewicz
Design & Prepress Manager: Anne-Michelle Gallero
Brand Manager: Jonathan White
Associate Prepress Manager: Alex Voznesenskiy
Associate Production Manager: Kimberly Marshall
Assistant Brand Manager: Stephanie Braga

Editorial Director: Stephen Koepp

Special thanks: Katherine Barnet, Jeremy Biloon, Rose Cirrincione, Lorin Driggs, Jacqueline Fitzgerald, Christine Font, Jenna Goldberg, Hillary Hirsch, David Kahn, Amy Mangus, Amy Migliaccio, Nina Mistry, Jonathan Rosenbloom, Dave Rozzelle, Ricardo Santiago, Adriana Tierno, Elizabeth Winchester, Vanessa Wu

For information on TIME FOR KIDS magazine for the classroom or home, go to TIMEFORKIDS.COM or call 1-800-777-8600.
For subscriptions to SI KIDS, go to SIKIDS.COM or call 1-800-889-6007.

Published by TIME FOR KIDS Books, an imprint of Time Home Entertainment Inc.
135 West 50th Street
New York, NY 10020

ISBN 10: 1-61893-042-7
ISBN 13: 978-1-61893-042-2
Library of Congress Control Number: 2013932156

TIME FOR KIDS is a trademark of Time Inc.

We welcome your comments and suggestions about TIME FOR KIDS Books. Please write to us at: TIME FOR KIDS Books, Attention: Book Editors, P.O. Box 11016, Des Moines, IA 50336-1016
If you would like to order any of our hardcover Collector's Edition books, please call us at 1-800-327-6388 (Monday through Friday, 7 a.m. to 8 p.m., or Saturday, 7 a.m. to 6 p.m., Central Time).

1 QGT 13

Contents

HOW to Use This Book

Have you ever wondered where electricity comes from? Or where you can find the most poisonous snake? Do you know where you can find an asteroid magnet? The *Big Book of Where* has the answers to these questions—and many more you may never have thought to ask. In 10 chapters, you'll travel from the comforts of home to each of the seven continents, dive deep into the oceans, and even venture out into the solar system. Along the way, you'll discover some surprising facts that you can use to impress your friends—like where you can find the world's original "bungee jumpers," the oldest mummies, and a 3,300-mile-long fence. Check out the glossary at the end of the book to find out the meaning of some words and terms.

Explanation: Here's where you'll find detailed answers to the question at the top of the page.

Locator Globes: Show you where in the world.

Photos: Colorful pictures make the facts and figures come alive.

Information Boxes: Short sidebars expand the topic and lead you to other parts of the world.

WHERE is the longest fence in the world?

Australia's Dingo Barrier Fence twists and turns its way across more than 3,300 miles of Australia. The fence protects southeastern Australia from dingoes, or wild dogs.

When European settlers began to arrive in Australia, they brought along animals like rabbits and sheep. To the dingoes, these animals were a great new food source. No one minded that dingoes killed rabbits because there were so many of them. In fact, fences were built to try to keep the rabbits from spreading throughout the country. But killing sheep *was* a problem because people raised them for money.

The government tried to help by putting a bounty on dingoes: paying people to kill them. In 1948, the government suggested building the Dingo Barrier Fence. The wire mesh barrier is six feet high and extends another foot underground. It does a pretty good job of keeping out the dingoes, but it requires constant upkeep. And not everyone is happy about the fence. Some people think it should be torn down. Without dingoes around, the numbers of rats, foxes, and other imported animals that eat or compete with native animals explode. Where there are dingoes, those animals are kept in check and the native plants and animals have a better chance to survive.

Ships of the Australian Outback

Camels were brought to Australia as working animals in the 1800s because much of the country is dry and camels can go for a long time with little water. When trucks replaced them, the camels were freed. Now there are more wild camels in Australia than anywhere else. Like other imported species, the camels compete with native animals for food and water. They can also kill plants and trees by eating all their leaves. This becomes a real problem when a dust storm kicks up and there's not enough plant life left to hold the soil in place.

Invasion of the Melaleuca

An alien species is threatening to take over Florida's Everglades and endangering the native plants. It's the melaleuca tree, a native of Australia. It grows fast and high, and just one full-grown tree can produce up to 100 million seeds. Without animals or pests to feed on it, the melaleuca took over as much as 20% of the undeveloped land in southern Florida. Since 1997, however, two Australian bugs have been set loose and are chowing down on the melaleuca trees, which are their favorite food. Luckily, the bugs aren't interested in American plants.

Maps: Zero in on particular places.

Color border: Different color borders let you quickly see what chapter you're in.

1

Home

Where do you live? It's a question that can be answered in many ways. You can say that you live in the Milky Way galaxy, or on Planet Earth, or in North or South America or Africa, in the United States or India, in a city or on a farm, in a house or an apartment. Wherever you live, it's the place you call home.

People who live in farmhouses often don't have neighbors close by.

In cities, many people live in tall apartment buildings.

The Uros people of South America live in reed houses built on artificial reed islands in Lake Titicaca.

Some people live in mobile homes—even if they never move them.

In Mongolia, some people live in *gers* (also called yurts), tent-like homes made of felt stretched over a wood frame. If you want to move, you can collapse your *ger* and take it with you!

WHERE does your electricity come from?

Flipping a switch may be easy, but it's only the last step in getting electricity to turn on the lights, the TV, the computer, and most appliances in your home. But where does electricity come from and how does it get to the switch?

Electricity is produced in power plants. Most of the plants use fuel, such as coal, natural gas, nuclear power, or garbage, to boil water. The steam from the hot water spins large blades in engines called turbines to create energy. Another machine, called a generator, turns the mechanical energy produced by the turbines into electricity. In hydroelectric plants, water is used to turn the turbines. Solar energy, wind power, and geothermal energy—heat created deep inside Earth—can also be used to create electricity.

After the electricity has been produced, it goes through transformers that increase the voltage, or intensity. This high-voltage electricity is then sent through long-distance cables to substations. There, it goes through more transformers, this time to lower the voltage.

The electricity leaves the substation through power lines. Smaller transformers on utility poles or in boxes lower the voltage even more until the electricity is safe to use in your home.

On the way into your house, the electricity runs through a meter that measures how much you use.

Next, it goes through a fuse box or circuit breaker that keeps the house safe in case an appliance causes a short circuit, or sudden accidental surge of electricity. From there, it passes through wires in the walls to the switches and electrical outlets.

That's Hair-raising!

Has your hair ever stood on end after you comb it? Static electricity is the culprit. Electricity is produced when the positive charges (protons) and negative charges (electrons) in an atom get out of balance. When the comb rubs against your hair, electrons jump from your hair to the comb. The protons left in your hair push away from each other—and your hair stands on end. The same thing can happen when you rub your hair with a balloon.

WHERE do the most germs hide out?

Germs is the word often used for microbes (living things you can't see without a microscope) that can make you sick. Bacteria are among the most common germs. They can cause problems such as stomach cramps, nausea, diarrhea, tonsillitis, strep throat, cavities, and ear infections. So where will you find the most bacteria in a home? In the kitchen. Sponges and dishcloths, sinks and faucet handles, cutting boards, stove knobs, pet dishes, and countertops can all harbor germs. Other germy hotspots in the house include toothbrush holders, shower curtains, TV remotes, doorknobs, and light switches.

Cleanliness is the best way to keep bacteria from making you sick. First, wash your hands with regular soap and warm water—often! Do it before handling food or eating and after handling food (especially raw foods like meat), going to the bathroom, blowing your nose, coughing, sneezing, petting or cleaning up after your pet, taking out the trash, or any time you may pick up bacteria. Surfaces can be cleaned up with a cleanser that also disinfects. Dishcloths can go in the laundry and wet sponges (without metal parts) can be zapped for two minutes in the microwave. Dirty pet dishes or toothbrush holders can go in the dishwasher or be washed by hand in warm, soapy water.

Body Bugs

Scientists say there are 10 times as many cells from bacteria and other microbes in the body than there are human cells! These bacteria can be good or bad—or both—depending on where they are and whether they're in a healthy situation. For example, when your mouth is healthy, good bacteria can keep bad bacteria in check. But if you have poor eating habits, your mouth may become "friendlier" to the bad bacteria that can cause cavities or gum disease.

Going Viral

Viruses are germs, too, and they are even smaller than bacteria. Viruses can't survive for long unless they're in a living creature. But once they're in, they can cause colds, flu, chickenpox, and measles. Viruses often spread through the air. If someone with a cold or the flu coughs or sneezes, they release droplets that may contain the virus. Someone standing nearby may breathe in those droplets—and the virus.

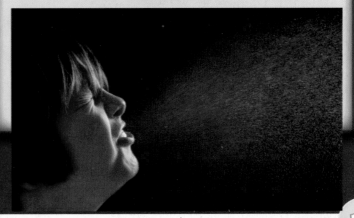

WHERE does your trash go?

If you're like most people, you put your trash in garbage cans. Then, once or twice a week, trucks take it away. But what happens to it? After your garbage is picked up, the truck squishes it all together to fit as much inside as possible. When the truck is full, the garbage is dropped off at a transfer station. But the trash doesn't stay there for long. Large tractor-trailer trucks collect the garbage and haul it to a landfill.

After the trash is dumped into the landfill, bulldozers and other heavy equipment roll back and forth over the mounds of garbage to compress them so they can squeeze more in. When all the day's garbage has been compressed, it's covered over with a layer of dirt. Landfills are better than open dumps, but they don't get rid of the garbage. They only hide it.

Basically, a landfill is a big hole built into the ground and lined with clay, plastic, and fabric to keep any liquids or chemicals from seeping into the groundwater. At the bottom are drainage layers of gravel and sand. A system of pumps and pipes collects any nasty liquids that may filter down through the garbage. Other pipes collect methane gas that can be used to make electricity. The soil and water near a landfill have to be checked often for pollution—even up to 30 years after the landfill is closed.

The Breakdown

Very little air, water, or light gets into landfills, so it takes a long time for the garbage to decompose, or break down. But whether they're in a landfill or not, some kinds of trash just don't break down easily. One kind is plastic. No one knows exactly how long plastics can last, but some experts think it could be hundreds of years, at least. Glass can last even longer—and there's evidence. Scientists have found glass beads that date back more than 5,500 years!

These Egyptian beads have survived more than 3,000 years!

Too Much Trash!

The U.S. produces more trash than any other country in the world: 250 million tons a year. That's a big number to wrap your mind around, so think of it this way: Each American produces about 4.4 pounds of garbage every day, or 1,606 pounds a year. Just over half of all that trash is discarded, and the rest gets recycled or burned.

Breakdown Times for Litter

Here's how long the U.S. National Park Service says it can take for different kinds of litter to break down.

1. Glass bottle: 1 million years

2. Plastic fishing line: 600 years

3. Plastic drink bottle: 450 years

4. Aluminum can: 80–200 years

5. Foam plastic buoy: 80 years

WHERE does your water come from?

Without fresh water, there would be no life on Earth. Even if you already knew that, you may still take water for granted. And why not? You and your family can probably get all the water you need—for drinking, cooking, washing dishes and clothes, showering, watering the lawn—just by turning on a tap. Where does all that water come from?

The water you use in your home comes from a lake, river, or aquifer (*ak*-wuh-fur)—an underground layer of porous rock, sand, or gravel. If you don't have your own private well, you get your water through a public water system.

On the way to your home, the water travels through pipes to a treatment plant. There, dirt and other pollutants are removed from the water, and small amounts of chemicals such as chlorine (to kill germs) and fluoride (to help prevent tooth decay) are added.

Once the water reaches your home, it goes through a water meter (to keep track of how much you use) and into the plumbing system of your house.

This complicated system of pipes, drains, traps (the U-shaped part of pipes leading to sinks and tubs), and vents supplies water to your water heater, sink, tub and shower, toilet, dishwasher, clothes washer, outdoor faucets—wherever you need it.

Supply and Demand

Although water covers more than 70% of our planet, only 3% of that is fresh water. In the U.S., 400 billion gallons of fresh water are used every day. About half of that goes to generating electricity. Fresh water is also needed for farming, ranching, and industry as well as for home use. Many people worry about having enough fresh water for future needs. That's why it's important to learn about all the ways there are to save water.

Walking for Water

Not everyone is lucky enough to have clean running water. In fact, almost half of all the people in the world don't have water piped into their homes. Of these, about 780 million people don't even have access to safe drinking water. Most live in rural areas of Asia, Oceania, and sub-Saharan Africa (south of the Sahara Desert). In some parts of Africa, people—usually women and girls—have to walk for miles to find a water source, wait in line to get it, and then carry the water back home.

north America

A mother polar bear and her cub play on the ice while waiting for Hudson Bay in Canada to freeze over.

Fiery volcanoes, frozen seas, snow-covered mountains, sunbaked deserts, vast wildernesses, crowded cities—just about every kind of environment on Earth can be found in North America, the third largest continent. Although people say that Christopher Columbus "discovered" America in 1492, native peoples had been living there for thousands of years. By studying the genes of modern-day Native Americans, scientists have figured out that the first people probably arrived in the Americas as long as 30,000 years ago. They got there by crossing a land bridge that once connected Russia and Alaska.

About 3,000 years ago, the Olmec people of southeastern Mexico carved 9-foot-high stone heads from volcanic rock.

The spire of Mount Hayden overlooks the eastern end of Arizona's Grand Canyon.

RUSSIA

Bering Sea

Nome
Bethel
Barrow
Prudhoe Bay

ARCTIC OCEAN

Aleutian Islands

Alaska (U.S.)
Fairbanks
Anchorage
Kodiak
Valdez

Beaufort Sea

Inuvik

Banks Island

Kaujuitoq Resolute

Victoria Island

Echo Bay

Arctic Circle

Queen Elizabeth Islands

Alert

Qaanaaq (Thule)

GREENLAND
(Denmark)

Greenland Sea

ICELAND

Baffin Bay

Baffin Island

Davis Strait

Nuuk (Godthab)

Tasiilaq
(Ammassalik)

Narsarsuaq

Whitehorse
Juneau

Yellowknife

Igaluit

Labrador Sea

Churchill

HUDSON BAY

Edmonton
Calgary

Vancouver
Victoria
Olympia Seattle
Salem Portland

Saskatoon

Regina

Winnipeg

Chisasibi
(Fort George)

Moosonee

CANADA

Happy Valley
Goose Bay

Island of Newfoundland
St. John's

Boise
Helena

Bismarck

Pierre

Saint-Pierre

San Francisco
Sacramento Carson City

Cheyenne

Minneapolis St. Paul
Madison

Quebec
Fredericton
Charlottetown

Salt Lake City
Denver

Omaha Des Moines
Lincoln

Milwaukee
Chicago

Detroit
Toledo

Toronto

Montreal
Montpelier
Ottawa

Halifax

Los Angeles
San Diego
Tijuana

UNITED STATES

Phoenix
Santa Fe

Kansas City
Topeka
Jefferson City

Springfield
Indianapolis

Cleveland

Buffalo
Albany

Pittsburgh
Harrisburg

Concord Augusta
Boston

Hartford Providence
New York

Saint Louis

Cincinnati
Frankfort
Louisville

Baltimore
Philadelphia
Dover

Washington, D.C.

ATLANTIC OCEAN

Ciudad Juárez El Paso
Hermosillo

Oklahoma City

Dallas

Memphis
Little Rock
Nashville

Charleston
Richmond
Norfolk
Raleigh

Tropic of Cancer

MEXICO

Gulf of California

Monterrey

San Antonio
Austin

Houston

Baton Rouge
New Orleans

Birmingham Atlanta
Jackson
Montgomery

Columbia

Savannah

Hamilton
BERMUDA (U.K.)

Tallahassee
Jacksonville

La Paz

Mazatlán

Tampico

GULF OF MEXICO

Freeport
Miami

Puerto Vallarta

León

Mérida
Cancún

Nassau

BAHAMAS

TURKS AND CAICOS ISLANDS
(U.K.)

VIRGIN ISLANDS
(U.S., U.K.)

Guadalajara
Mexico City
Puebla

Havana

CUBA

Grand Turk

**SAINT MAARTEN/
SAINT MARTIN**
(Netherlands)/(France)

Acapulco

Veracruz

Oaxaca

Camagüey

CAYMAN ISLANDS (U.K.)

George Town

DOMINICAN REPUBLIC

Puerto Rico (U.S.)

ANGUILLA
(U.K.)

SAINT BARTHELEMY
(France)

PACIFIC OCEAN

Belmopan Belize City

BELIZE

Guantánamo
Montego Bay

JAMAICA

Kingston

HAITI

Port-au-Prince

San Juan

Santo Domingo

Santiago

SAINT KITTS AND NEVIS

MONTSERRAT (U.K.)

GUADELOUPE (France)

ANTIGUA AND BARBUDA

DOMINICA

MARTINIQUE (France)

Guatemala City

GUATEMALA

HONDURAS

Tegucigalpa

CARIBBEAN SEA

CURAÇAO
(Neth.)

BONAIRE
(Neth.)

SAINT LUCIA

BARBADOS

San Salvador
EL SALVADOR

NICARAGUA

Managua

ARUBA (Neth.)

**SAINT VINCENT AND
THE GRENADINES**

GRENADA

TRINIDAD AND TOBAGO

COSTA RICA

San José
Panama City

PANAMA

COLOMBIA

VENEZUELA

SOUTH AMERICA

GUYANA

0 mi   500 mi   1,000 mi

0 km   500 km   1,000 km

WHERE did Columbus first set foot in the New World?

On October 10, 1492, the sailors on the *Niña*, *Pinta*, and *Santa Maria* were angry and ready to mutiny. They had been at sea for more than a month and still hadn't found land. Their captain, Christopher Columbus, calmed them down, but who knew how long the peace would last? Two nights later, land was sighted!

When daylight came, the Spanish explorers saw people on the beach. Columbus took a few of his men and went ashore. When he landed, he gave a prayer of thanksgiving and claimed the land for Spain. In his log, Columbus described the native people as handsome and friendly. Although they called the island Guanahani, Columbus renamed it San Salvador.

Columbus was sure he had reached Asia, but in fact he had landed on an island in the Bahamas. Experts disagree on exactly which one, and at least nine islands have been suggested. Given Columbus's route, the two places that seem most likely are present-day San Salvador and Samana Cay. However, in his journal, Columbus said that Guanahani had a large lake in the middle, and only San Salvador—which was called Watling Island from the 1600s to 1926—matches this description.

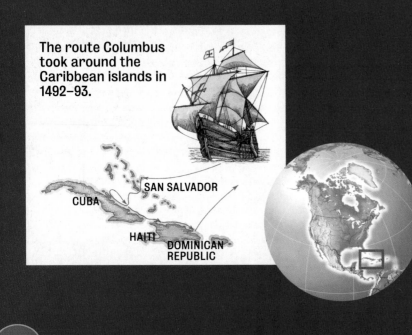

The route Columbus took around the Caribbean islands in 1492–93.

SAN SALVADOR

CUBA

HAITI

DOMINICAN REPUBLIC

Stone-Age Explorers?

Christopher Columbus and his men were not the first Europeans to reach the Americas. Up until now, that honor has gone to Leif Eriksson and his fellow Vikings, who sailed west from Greenland to Newfoundland, Canada, almost 500 years earlier. But today, some scientists say that the first Europeans may have arrived in the New World more than 20,000 years ago. They base their theory on stone tools found on the East Coast of the U.S. that look a lot like European tools of the Stone Age.

A statue of Leif Eriksson in Greenland

Going Places

After Christopher Columbus, many European explorers headed to the Americas. The first wave included John Cabot, who explored the northeastern coast of North America in 1497–98. In 1513, Vasco Núñez Balboa crossed the Isthmus of Panama and reached the Pacific Ocean, and Juan Ponce de León explored Florida. In 1519, Hernán Cortés (right) landed in Mexico and conquered the Aztecs. And in 1520, Ferdinand Magellan was first to find a sea route from the Atlantic to the Pacific.

WHERE was the Spanish Main?

The Spanish Main refers to the routes of Spanish ships trading with Spain's colonies in the Caribbean Sea, the Gulf of Mexico, and the Atlantic Ocean along the Florida coast. Twice a year, a convoy, or fleet, of up to 90 ships sailed from Spain with supplies for the Spanish colonists. But it was on the return trip, when the ships were loaded with gold, silver, gems, furs, sugar, and other valuables from the New World, that they were in danger from pirates and privateers.

Privateers were legal pirates, licensed by the English, French, and Dutch governments to raid enemy ships. One of the Dutch privateers, Piet Heyn, commanded a fleet of 36 ships. In 1628, he did what no other privateer or pirate had ever managed. He captured the entire cargo of a Spanish treasure fleet carrying gold and silver worth about seven billion dollars in today's money.

Blackbeard

For two years, Edward Teach, better known as Blackbeard, hid along the coast of North Carolina and attacked merchant ships. Blackbeard believed in dressing the part of a pirate. He carried six pistols slung on belts across his chest. He wore his black beard in pigtails tied with ribbons and stuck slow-burning cannon fuses under his hat so his head would be surrounded by smoke! In 1718, the British navy caught up with Blackbeard and he was wounded 25 times before he died. Then the British cut off his head and hung it from a naval ship.

Gulf of
Mexico

SPAIN

Atlantic
Ocean

Usually two treasure fleets sailed from
Spain. After a stop in the Canary Islands
off the coast of Africa, they crossed the
Atlantic Ocean. One fleet sailed to South
and Central America (white), and the other
fleet went to Mexico (yellow). The two
fleets met up in Havana, Cuba. Together,
they sailed north along the coast of Florida
before heading back to Spain (red).

Women Pirates

Although the pirate code barred
females, a few women dressed like
men and joined pirate crews. Two
of the most famous were Anne
Bonny and Mary Read, who sailed
the Caribbean with Calico Jack
Rackham. When Rackham's ship
was captured in 1720, both women
were sentenced to hang but neither
did. Read died of a fever in prison
and Bonny was set free.

WHERE are the highest tides in the world?

High tides in Canada's Bay of Fundy can reach about 56 feet—higher than a 5-story building. The funnel-shaped bay becomes narrower and shallower along its length, forcing the water higher and higher up the shore. At the head of the bay, Minas Basin has the highest tides.

The length of the tidal cycle—one high tide and one low tide—is 12 hours and 26 minutes. So twice a day, more than 120 billion tons of water flow in and out of the 174-mile-long bay. That's equal to the daily flow of water in all the rivers of the world combined!

Surging tides stir up nutrients from the seafloor and marshes, providing food for an incredible number of animals, from sea slugs to fish, seals, whales, and more than 300 species of birds. Among these are millions of migrating seabirds that flock to the bay's mudflats to dine on tiny animals called mud shrimp.

Tourists also flock to the Bay of Fundy. They go to see the changing tides and whirlpools, to explore the mudflats and look at the sea stacks shaped by the tides, to hunt fossils, and to enjoy bird- and whale-watching.

At low tide, people can walk around sea stacks carved by the ocean. But they have to be careful not to get caught there when the tide comes in (top right).

A surfer rides a tidal bore in Brazil.

Surfing the Tides

Tidal bores are surf-like waves that form when an incoming tide forces a river to flow upstream. Only about 100 rivers in the world have tidal bores. With waves reaching almost 30 feet high and traveling up to 25 mph, the Silver Dragon tidal bore on China's Qiantang River is the largest. The strongest is on the Amazon River in Brazil, where waves can reach 13 feet high and flow far inland. Tidal bores have become popular spots for surfers to try their skills.

WHERE was the bloodiest battle of the Civil War fought?

GETTYSBURG.

On July 1, 1863, the Confederate Army under General Robert E. Lee invaded the North. In the early morning of July 1, Lee's army attacked Union forces at Gettysburg, Pennsylvania. After a full day of fighting, the Confederates took the town, and Federal (Union) troops pulled back into the hills. The next day, Lee attacked the Union army again. Although the Confederates gained some ground, they could not move the Union forces from their hilltop positions.

On July 3, more fighting took place. When the battle was over, the Union had won. But the cost was great. In just three days, the Union and Confederate troops suffered more than 51,000 casualties—out of a total of about 165,000 soldiers. Of the casualties, more than 7,000 died and 33,000 were wounded. The rest were missing or captured.

Images of War

Without the speed and smaller size of today's handheld cameras, Civil War photographers couldn't take pictures during battles. But they could photograph the battlefields, graves, and ruins left behind. For the first time in history, photos brought the reality of war to people who live far away from the battlefields.

This photograph shows the ruins of a railroad depot in Richmond, Virginia, in 1865.

Angel of the Battlefield

Clara Barton and her helpers provided wagonloads of food, clothing, and medical supplies as well as comfort and care to soldiers in field hospitals. But they also risked their lives to help the wounded while fighting raged around them. After the war, Barton helped identify the graves of nearly 13,000 Union soldiers who died at Andersonville, a Confederate prisoner-of-war camp. She later founded the American Red Cross to provide aid following natural disasters and during wartime.

Short and Sweet

It only took President Abraham Lincoln two minutes to give the Gettysburg Address, one of the greatest speeches of all time. In it, he said that "these dead shall not have died in vain; that the nation shall have a new birth of freedom, and that government of the people, by the people, for the people, shall not perish from the earth."

A handwritten draft of Lincoln's speech

WHERE was the largest Maya city?

Long before Spanish explorers sailed to the New World, the Maya people had a great civilization. Their largest city was Tikal in northern Guatemala, Central America. First settled about 2,600 years ago, the city was at its greatest between A.D. 700 and 800, when more than 60,000 people lived there. Within 100 years, Tikal, like other cities of the Maya, was largely abandoned.

Almost 1,000 years later, explorers heard rumors of a lost city whose towers seemed to float above the rain forest. In 1848, they set out to find it. Since then, archaeologists have slowly been freeing the overgrown city from the jungle and uncovering its secrets.

Scientists have found the ruins of about 3,000 buildings. Six of them are steep-sided step pyramids, including one more than 20 stories high. In the center of the city, two pyramids face each other across a wide plaza. On the north side are more than 100 temples. Rulers were buried in temple tombs with pottery, ornaments, and other objects. To the south of the plaza are more temples, palaces, and reservoirs that held drinking water. Wide avenues connect the city center to the two farthest pyramids. And, like suburbs, homes were built all around the city.

Tikal's Great Plaza and one of its two step pyramids. Stelae are lined up in front of the steps and the temple ruins on the left.

Maya Masks

Many of Tikal's buildings were decorated with carvings, including 10-foot-tall masks of Maya gods. This one is Chac, the god of rain.

Stories in Stone

The Maya had a written language with hieroglyphic symbols for both words and sounds. Stone slabs called stelae (steelee) were carved with images of gods or rulers on one side. On the other side, hieroglyphs gave the names of rulers and described their accomplishments. In Tikal, scientists have found the names of 33 rulers, including at least one woman.

WHERE is Silicon Valley?

Silicon Valley is one of the world's major centers of high-tech industry. It includes the southern San Francisco Bay area and the Santa Clara Valley in California. The term Silicon Valley was first used in 1971. "Silicon" comes from the material used to make computer chips, and "Valley" comes from the Santa Clara Valley.

The area's high-tech history goes way back to 1939, when William Hewlett and David Packard started their business in a garage in Palo Alto, California. Today, Hewlett-Packard is a multibillion-dollar firm making computers, printers, and other technological equipment. Of course, it's not the only well-known company in Silicon Valley. Others include Apple, Google, Facebook, Intel, and eBay, to name just a few.

The restored garage where Hewlett and Packard started their business in 1939.

At Google offices there are plenty of toys and video games—as well as whiteboards for writing down new ideas.

Growing Fast

Home to Microsoft and Amazon, the region around Seattle, Washington, is one of the fastest-growing technology centers in the United States.

A microprocessor chip made by Intel

Facebook Friends

Mark Zuckerberg launched Facebook from his dormitory room in 2004. Soon after, he moved the offices to Silicon Valley. The social network giant has more than a billion users around the world.

WHERE is the North Pole?

Now that's a tricky question. There are four North Poles—and three of them move around. The one that doesn't move is the **geographic** North Pole (shown on the map). That's where all the lines of longitude (the north-south lines on a map) come together in the ice-covered Arctic Ocean.

If you imagine Earth spinning around an axle, or rod, the **instantaneous** North Pole would be where one end of the axle meets the surface. Because Earth wobbles as it rotates on its axis, the instantaneous North Pole moves in a tight, irregular circle around the geographic North Pole.

The needle of your compass points to the **magnetic** North Pole. The magnetic North Pole has been slowly moving north across Canada's Nunavut territory. In 1989, it started to speed up and is now heading across the Arctic Ocean toward Siberia at about 40 miles per year.

The **geomagnetic** North Pole marks the axis of Earth's magnetic field. This pole is moving north, too, but much more slowly than the magnetic pole. It is currently located on the northeast side of Canada's Ellesmere Island.

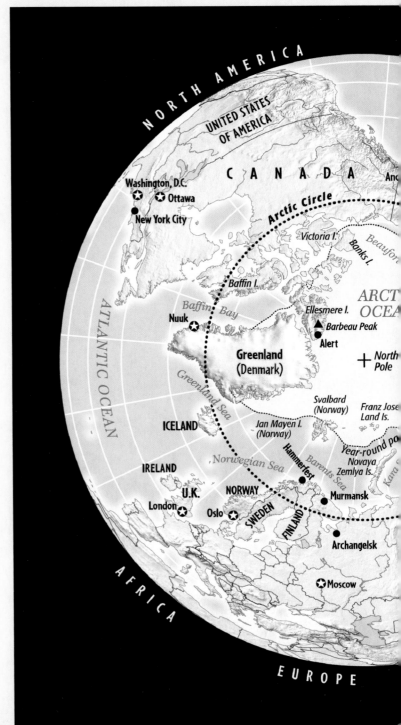

Dear Santa

Ever wonder what happens to all those letters kids write to Santa Claus? Lots of them end up at the post office in North Pole, Alaska, a small town near Fairbanks. The town is nowhere near any of the actual North Poles.

Why Do the Magnetic Poles Move?

Earth has a solid inner core surrounded by an outer core of liquid iron and other metals. Scientists think the magnetic field is caused by electrical currents created in the outer core by the roiling movement of the superhot liquid metal (think of water boiling in a pot) combined with the rotation of Earth. Since the source of the magnetic field is always in motion, it's not surprising that the poles move, too.

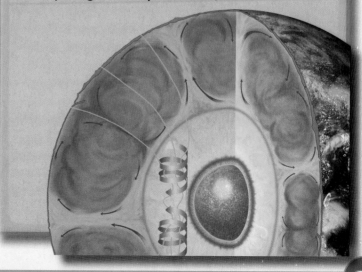

WHERE was the phrase "rock and roll" first used?

In 1951, disk jockey Alan Freed launched the *Moondog Show* on the WJW radio station in Cleveland, Ohio. He played "blues and rhythm records" by African-American performers like Gil Bernal, Kitty Noble, and the Dominoes. Some of the songs included words that Freed thought suited their "rolling, surging beat," and it wasn't long before he gave the music a new name—rock and roll. The name stuck and so did the music, which over the years has evolved into the rock music of today.

Freed also tried to have a Moondog Coronation Ball. On March 21, 1952, more than 10,000 people jammed the old Cleveland Arena, with thousands more trying to get in. The fire department was worried about overcrowding, so they stopped the concert almost as soon as it began. Even so, the Moondog Coronation Ball is considered to be the first major rock concert.

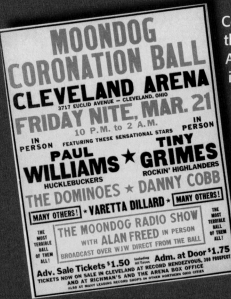

MOONDOG CORONATION BALL
CLEVELAND ARENA
3717 EUCLID AVENUE – CLEVELAND, OHIO
FRIDAY NITE, MAR. 21
10 P.M. to 2 A.M.
IN PERSON FEATURING THESE SENSATIONAL STARS IN PERSON
PAUL WILLIAMS ★ TINY GRIMES
HUCKLEBUCKERS ROCKIN' HIGHLANDERS
THE DOMINOES ★ DANNY COBB
MANY OTHERS! ★ VARETTA DILLARD ★ MANY OTHERS!
THE MOST TERRIBLE BALL OF THEM ALL!
THE MOONDOG RADIO SHOW
WITH ALAN FREED IN PERSON
BROADCAST OVER WJW DIRECT FROM THE BALL
THE MOST TERRIBLE BALL OF THEM ALL!
Adv. Sale Tickets $1.50 Including All Taxes   Adm. at Door $1.75
TICKETS NOW ON SALE IN CLEVELAND AT RECORD RENDEZVOUS, 300 PROSPECT
AND AT RICHMAN'S AND THE ARENA BOX OFFICE
ALSO AT MANY LEADING RECORD SHOPS IN OTHER NORTHERN OHIO CITIES

Alan Freed

Early Rock and Roll

1951
Alan Freed promotes pop music as rock and roll on his Cleveland, Ohio, radio show

1952
Moondog Coronation Ball, the first major rock concert

1955
Bill Haley's "Rock Around the Clock" is the first rock-and-roll song to top the charts

1956
Elvis Presley sings "Hound Dog" on TV and shocks viewers with the way he wiggles his hips

Dancing to the Beat

In Philadelphia, Pennsylvania, a local TV dance show got a new host in 1956. His name was Dick Clark, and just a year later, *American Bandstand* went national on the ABC network. Teenagers danced to rock and roll and rated the songs—giving rise to a popular expression: "It's got a good beat and you can dance to it."

Rock On

More than 275 rock-and-roll greats from past and present are honored at the Rock and Roll Hall of Fame and Museum, which opened in Cleveland, Ohio, in 1995.

1957
Dick Clark's TV show *American Bandstand* goes national

1960
Chubby Checker (left) sings "The Twist" and starts a dance craze

1961
The Shirelles are the first female group to top the charts with "Will You Still Love Me Tomorrow"

1964
Five singles by the British group, the Beatles, hold the top five spots on the U.S. charts—at the same time

WHERE was the first basketball game played?

At the YMCA Training School in Springfield, Massachusetts, students had to take gym class for an hour every day. When the weather was good and they could be outside, the young men had a great time. But in the winter, they were stuck with inside exercises and games that they didn't enjoy. In 1891, the gym teacher, James Naismith, was told by his supervisor to come up with an indoor game that would be fun for the students—and keep them out of trouble.

Naismith remembered Duck on a Rock, a childhood game that involved throwing stones. Clearly, rocks wouldn't do, but a soccer ball would work. To cut down on rough play, Naismith came up with 13 rules. One rule was that players couldn't run with the ball. Another disallowed "shouldering, holding, pushing, or striking."

On the big day, Naismith nailed two peach baskets to the bottom of a balcony on each side of the gym. Then he chose two men as captains, had each one pick his team, and tossed the soccer ball up in the air between two players. It was December 21, 1891, and the first basketball game was in play.

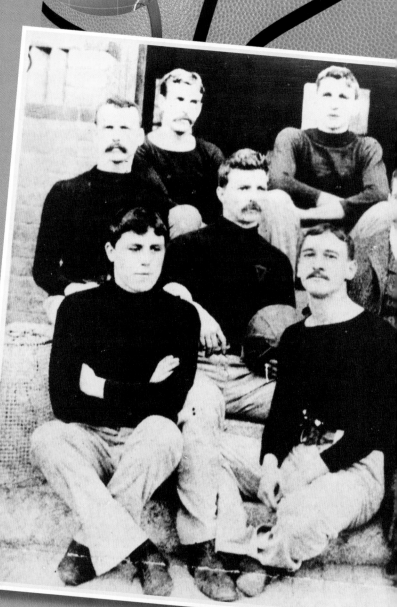

James Naismith (center right) with the first basketball team

Women of the Court

Senda Berenson taught gym at Smith College in Northampton, Massachusetts. She heard about basketball and went to see it played. Although many people at the time didn't think team sports for women were a good idea, Berenson decided to teach the game to her students. And on March 22, 1893, first- and second-year college students played the first women's championship basketball game to a full house.

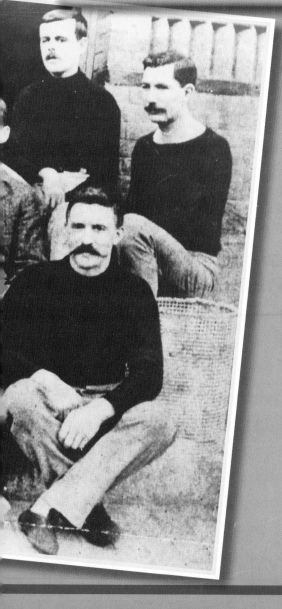

During the 1961–62 National Basketball Association (NBA) season, Wilt Chamberlain of the then Philadelphia Warriors scored 4,029 points—a record that still stands.

WHERE was the first capital of the United States?

It was summer 1788. Eleven out of 13 states had ratified the Constitution. Now it was time to put it into operation. But where should the capital of the young United States be located? Some members of the Congress argued for Philadelphia or Lancaster, Pennsylvania, or for Annapolis or Baltimore, Maryland. Other members fought for the new seat of government to be in the same place where they were already meeting. They won the argument, and New York City became the first capital.

The first Federal Congress met at the newly remodeled Federal Hall on Wall Street on March 4, 1789. However, the weather was bad and not enough senators and representatives had arrived to conduct business. It was another month before everyone could gather and count the electoral votes for the nation's first President. With 69 out of 138 votes, George Washington became the country's leader. John Adams, with the second-highest number of votes, became Vice President.

On April 30, 1789, Washington took the oath of office on the balcony of Federal Hall. Eliza Quincy, an eyewitness, wrote that "the windows and the roofs of the houses were crowded, and in the streets the throng was so dense that it seemed as if one might literally walk on the heads of the people." After Washington was sworn in, a 13-cannon salute was fired and "All the bells in the city rang out a peal of joy."

This print shows George Washington taking the oath of office at New York City's Federal Hall.

Congress Hall in Philadelphia

A New Capital

The southern states didn't want the capital in New York, a northern state that did not allow slavery. To keep these states from breaking up the Union, Congress passed the Residence Act in 1790. This law provided for a new capital to be located along the Potomac River between Maryland and Virginia, two slave states. While it was being built, the temporary capital would be moved farther south to Philadelphia, Pennsylvania.

A Capital Plan

After George Washington chose a place for the permanent capital, he hired French architect Pierre L'Enfant to design it. There was not enough money or time to realize L'Enfant's grand plans. But enough buildings were completed—including the White House—for the new city of Washington, D.C., to become the nation's capital in 1800.

One of the first photos of the White House, in 1846

WHERE is the oldest city in the Western Hemisphere?

People have lived in Mexico City since 1325, when the Aztecs founded their capital city of Tenochtitlán. By the 1500s, more than 200,000 people lived there—more than in most European cities of the time. When the Spanish conquistadors, or conquerors, arrived in 1519, they were dazzled by Tenochtitlán's brightly painted pyramids and shining white palaces. They were even more dazzled by Aztec gold. Within a year, the Spanish had conquered the Aztecs, destroyed their city, and begun building a new one on its ruins.

Today, more than 20 million people live in Mexico City and its suburbs, making it one of the world's largest metro areas. It's also the capital of Mexico and the center of the country's business and culture. Modern skyscrapers rise above colonial buildings, like the Metropolitan Cathedral, begun in 1573 and completed 240 years later.

Located in a high valley, Mexico City is surrounded by even higher mountains that trap smog. In the 1980s, its air quality was among the worst in the world. Since then, the government has banned people from driving their cars one day a week, closed factories that polluted the air, and improved public transportation.

People flock to the Zócalo, a huge public square in the center of the old city, for festivals, concerts, and political events. On the north side stands the Metropolitan Cathedral.

The illustration shows how Tenochtitlán may have looked. The photograph shows the ruins of the main temple.

Number 1 in the U.S.

St. Augustine, Florida, is the oldest city founded by Europeans in the United States. It was named by the Spanish explorer Pedro Menéndez de Avilés in 1565. The city's Castillo de San Marcos was built in 1672. The fort's 30-foot-high, 12-foot-thick walls were built from coquina, a kind of limestone that has millions of tiny air pockets. Instead of shattering when struck by cannonballs, the coquina absorbed or deflected them.

WHERE were the transistor and microchip invented?

Before the transistor, vacuum tubes were used in circuits to amplify and control electric signals. But the tubes were large and slow, and quickly burned out. In 1947, at Bell Telephone Laboratories in Murray Hill, New Jersey, scientists Walter Brattain, John Bardeen, and William Shockley figured out how to make crystals perform the same job as vacuum tubes—and transistors were born.

Thanks to that discovery, electrical circuits using transistors could be small, but they still had to be made by hand. In late July 1947, Jack Kilby at Texas Instruments in Dallas had an idea. He thought that it would be easier and cheaper to produce circuits if all the parts were made out of the same material. By September, Kilby had built the first integrated circuit, or microchip. But handwork was still needed to attach the wires that connected the parts.

Just a few months later, Robert Noyce, an engineer at Fairchild Semiconductor in California, found a way to get rid of the wires. Instead, his microchip would use metal lines on top of a protective coating to connect the parts. For the chip, Noyce used silicon, which could handle more power without overheating.

Without these two inventions, there would be no smart phones, digital cameras, MP3 players, or laptop computers. Microchips and their transistors are in almost every electronic device there is, from musical greeting cards to spacecraft.

The first integrated circuit, shown enlarged at right

The ABC of Computers

The first electronic computer was built in 1941 at Iowa State College in Ames. It was called the Atanasoff-Berry Computer—or ABC—in honor of its inventors. In June, the two inventors showed the ABC to a scientist at the University of Pennsylvania. By 1945, a team there had built ENIAC (Electronic Numerical Integrator and Computer). ENIAC was patented as the first digital electronic computer. Almost 30 years later, it was proved that the basic ideas behind ENIAC came from the ABC.

Programmers using the ENIAC

Robert Noyce with a microchip diagram

South America

Soccer is the most popular sport in South America.

If you're looking for world records, South America is hard to beat. It has the world's longest mountain range, highest waterfall, largest tropical rain forest, and driest desert. And that's not all. It's also home to mummies that are older than the pyramids, penguins that live north of the equator, tiny frogs that are more poisonous than just about any other animal, snakes that grow up to 30 feet long, and spiders the size of dinner plates.

The Galapagos Islands of Ecuador are home to the marine iguana, the only lizard that gets its food from the sea.

Set high on a ridge in Peru, Machu Picchu was built by the Inca more than 500 years ago.

DOMINICAN
REPUBLIC
CUBA   Puerto Rico
                       (U.S.)
        HAITI   ANTIGUA AND
JAMAICA   BARBUDA
                SAINT KITTS
BELIZE   AND NEVIS   GUADELOUPE
HONDURAS   DOMINICA
        CARIBBEAN SEA   SAINT LUCIA   BARBADOS
NICARAGUA   GRENADA   SAINT VINCENT AND THE GRENADINES   ATLANTIC OCEAN
COSTA   Aruba   TRINIDAD
RICA   PANAMA   Barranquilla   Maracaibo   AND TOBAGO
                Cartagena   Caracas
                Lake   Orinoco River   Ciudad
                Maracaibo   Guayana   Georgetown
                    Medellín   Paramaribo
                                VENEZUELA   GUYANA   Cayenne
                    Bogotá   SURINAME   FRENCH
                Cali   GUIANA
                        COLOMBIA   Negro River   Macapá
        Esmeraldas   Belém   São Luís
Equator   Quito   Manaus   Amazon River   Parnaíba
ECUADOR   Santarém   Fortaleza
Galápagos Islands   Guayaquil   Iquitos   Benjamin   Madeira River   Natal
                            Constant   AMAZON
                    Amazon River   BASIN   Recife
            PERU   Piura   Selvas   Porto Velho   BRAZIL   Maceió
        Cruzeiro do Sul   San Francisco River
    Trujillo   Cobija   Brasília   Salvador
                        Riberalta
            Lima   Cusco   Brazilian
                    Lake   Highlands   Belo Horizonte
                    Titicaca   BOLIVIA
                Arequipa   La Paz   São Paulo
                    Cochabamba   Rio de Janeiro
                Arica   Santa Cruz   Curitiba
                    Sucre
                Iquique   PARAGUAY
                                    Asunción
            PACIFIC OCEAN   Antofagasta   Formosa   Ciudad
                                        del Este
                        San Miguel   Resistencia   Encarnación   Porto Alegre
                        de Tucumán
            CHILE   Córdoba   Salto
                                    URUGUAY   ATLANTIC OCEAN
                Valparaíso   Rosario
                Santiago   Buenos Aires   Montevideo
                                    Rio de la Plata
                Concepción   ARGENTINA   Mar del Plata

                            Bahía Blanca

                Puerto Montt

                                Comodoro Rivadavia

                            Strait of
                            Magellan
                    Río Gallegos   Stanley
            0 mi.   500 mi.   1,000 mi.   Punta Arenas   Falkland Is.
                            Ushuaia   (Islas Malvinas)
                                    (Administered by U.K.;
            0 km   500 km   1,000 km   Cape Horn   claimed by Argentina)

ANDES MTS
Magdalena River
Putumayo River
Marañón River
Ucayali River
Paraguay River
Paraná River
Kingu River
Tocantins River
Araguaia River

WHERE is the world's largest radio telescope array?

Chile's Chajnantor plateau in the Atacama Desert is high (about 3 miles above sea level), nearly cloudless, and far from city lights and radio signals. That means the air is crystal clear and perfect for stargazing. It's also perfect for ALMA, the world's largest set of radio telescopes. Even before it was completed in March 2013, ALMA was producing fantastic new images of the universe.

ALMA, which is short for Atacama Large Millimeter/submillimeter Array, is a set (array) of 66 telescopes, or dish antennas, each almost 40 feet in diameter. These huge telescopes work together to pick up weak radio waves that have been traveling through the universe for millions of years. The telescopes can detect wavelengths that are less than a millimeter. The signals are then sent over fiber-optic cables to a supercomputer. The computer combines and analyzes the information to create detailed images.

Each radio telescope sits on a docking pad. Although ALMA has only 66 telescopes, there are 192 docking pads. Fifty of the telescopes can be trucked from one docking pad to another to change their view of the sky. To map the gigantic nurseries where stars are born, the telescopes are placed close together. Smaller objects, such as a planet orbiting a distant sun, can be picked up more easily when the telescopes are placed farther apart.

Monster Trucks

ALMA's radio telescopes each weigh 115 tons, so it takes a big truck to move one around. Each of the two transporters, nicknamed Lore and Otto, weighs 130 tons, has 28 wheels, and is 33 feet wide, 66 feet long, and 20 feet high. Even though a transporter has an engine equal to two Formula One race cars, it can only crawl at 12 miles per hour when lugging a telescope.

A picture of the Antennae Galaxies by ALMA and the Hubble Space Telescope

PM-04

WHERE is the "Lost City of the Inca"?

In 1911, an 11-year-old Peruvian boy led American archaeologist Hiram Bingham to some ruins high on a ridge overlooking the Urubamba River in southeast Peru. When Bingham saw walls and terraces among the overgrowth, he was sure he'd discovered Vilcabamba, the fabled "Lost City of the Inca." Bingham held on to this belief until his death in 1957. In fact, he had found the ruins of a lost Inca city—just not the one he'd been looking for.

The city Bingham found was Machu Picchu, a masterpiece of Inca engineering. The remains of buildings and plazas stand on more than 700 walled terraces that were built to provide level areas. Beneath the terraces, a drainage system of crushed rock helps keep the city from slipping down the steep mountainside during the heavy rains between December and March. A water system channels spring water to fountains and baths.

Machu Picchu has stood for more than 500 years—even though no mortar was used in any of the walls. Instead, the stones were shaped and fit together so perfectly that even a knife blade can't slip between them. The walls, including doors and windows, tilt inward from bottom to top. When an earthquake hits, the stones "dance" around and then settle back into place.

The Real "Lost City"

Vilcabamba, Peru, was where the Inca made their last stand against the Spanish conquerors. After the city was destroyed in 1572, its site was forgotten. In 1964, two explorers found clues in old Spanish records that led them to an area northwest of Machu Picchu. There they found the overgrown ruins of a large city that later proved to be the real Vilcabamba.

Empire Building

Machu Picchu was probably built for an Incan king. At its most powerful, the empire stretched north from the capital of Cusco, Peru, into parts of what are now the nations of Ecuador, Colombia, Bolivia, Argentina, and Chile. The empire was connected by more than 14,000 miles of roads—some of which still exist.

The Inca believed that this special stone held the sun in its path across the sky.

WHERE can you find hundreds of huge thousand-year-old stone statues?

The San Agustín Archaeological Park covers more than 190 square miles in southwest Colombia. In the park are more than 400 megalithic (large stone) statues carved by the people who lived there from the first to eighth centuries A.D.

The San Agustín people used large blocks—more than 16 feet high—of soft volcanic rock to create images of people and animals. Most of the humanoid statues have large heads with exaggerated expressions. They often wear headdresses and earpieces. Traces of paint show that at least some of the statues were colored red, black, yellow, blue, and white.

The San Agustín people left no written records. All that is known about them is what scientists have gathered from studying the remains of their houses, stonework, and tombs.

The San Agustín area was probably a ceremonial center where

Stone statues of warriors and a god guard the entrance to a tomb.

chiefs were buried in stone tombs on artificial hilltop mounds. Often, three statues stand at the entrance of a tomb, the largest in the middle and a smaller one on either side. The walls of the tombs are decorated with carvings that were once painted.

After the eighth century, the San Agustín people stopped carving huge statues and building fancy tombs. The reason why is a mystery!

A statue in the shape of an eagle holds a snake in its beak and claws.

Stone Face

Huge stone figures ring the South Pacific island of Rapa Nui, or Easter Island, a territory of Chile. Between 400 and 600 years ago, the people who lived there carved statues, called moai (*moh*-eye), out of volcanic rock. They average more than 13 feet high and weigh almost 14 tons each. Almost 400 remain in the quarry where they were carved. Among them is the largest moai, which is almost 72 feet long and weighs about 45 tons.

WHERE did scientists find the world's oldest mummies?

When you hear the word mummy, you probably think of King Tut. But the oldest artificial mummies in the world were made by the Chinchorro people of the Atacama Desert in southern Peru and northern Chile. They began making mummies to preserve dead bodies about 7,000 years ago. That's more than 2,000 years before the Egyptians began to mummify their dead.

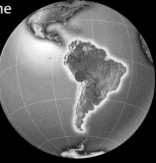

The Chinchorros lived along the Pacific coast. They were fishermen who used lines and fishhooks made of bone, shells, and cactus needles as well as woven nets. To hunt larger animals, they used harpoons and throwing sticks. About 5050 B.C., the Chinchorros in the Camarones Valley of Chile began to preserve their dead by mummification (photo left).

Scientists can learn about how mummies were made by studying them. The earliest Chinchorro mummy makers detached the skin, took the body apart, and removed the organs. After the bones had dried, they put them back together and tied them to long poles. They modeled new organs out of clay and replaced the muscles with reeds and sea grass. Then they stretched the skin back over the body and painted it with black manganese paste before adding a wig of short black hair.

Artificial mummies were preserved on purpose by people. Natural mummies are bodies accidentally preserved by the environment where they died. This timeline shows where some natural and artificial mummies have been found.

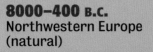

8000–400 B.C.
Northwestern Europe (natural)

5050–1700 B.C.
Chinchorro culture, Atacama Desert, northern Chile and southern Peru (artificial)

3000 B.C.–400 A.D.
Nile Valley, Egypt (artificial)

Chinchorro mummies come from every age and social class.

Ice Mummy

In 1995, the body of a teenage Inca girl was discovered near the top of Mount Ampato in Peru. She died more than 500 years ago and was naturally mummified when her body froze. Even her blood and stomach contents were preserved!

2000–1000 B.C.
Xinjiang, China (natural)

1000–400 B.C.
Pazyryk culture, Siberia (artificial)

1000–1400 A.D.
Guanche culture, Canary Islands (artificial)

1400–1532 A.D.
Inca culture, Peru and Chile (natural)

WHERE did Ferdinand Magellan find a passage from the Atlantic to the Pacific Ocean?

Portuguese navigator Ferdinand Magellan was sure he could find a waterway through South America. It would mean a new route to the Spice Islands (now the Moluccas of Indonesia). It would also mean a fortune trading in cloves, nutmeg, and other spices. In 1517, after a quarrel with the king of Portugal, Magellan took his idea to Charles I, the king of Spain.

At the time, the two countries were rivals and had drawn a line that divided the world between them. East of the line, trading routes and new discoveries belonged to Portugal. West of the line, they belonged to Spain. If Magellan found a western route, Spain would control it. Charles I liked that idea and gave Magellan five ships and enough money for a two-year trip.

In December 1519, Magellan's fleet began sailing slowly down the Atlantic coast of South America, searching for a passage to the other side. On October 21, 1520, Magellan finally entered a promising waterway.

As they sailed through the strait, the ships were tossed around by high tides, strong currents, and stormy waters. Finally, after 38 days and 350 miles, the crews sighted open water. Magellan had done it. He'd found a passage from the Atlantic to the Pacific Ocean. Although he called it the Channel of All Saints, the waterway was later named the Strait of Magellan.

Pacific Ocean

Ferdinand Magellan (1480–1521)

This satellite image shows the Strait of Magellan.

Atlantic Ocean

Antonio Pigafetta, a nobleman from Venice, kept a record of his voyage with Magellan. He also made hand-colored maps, including this one—the first map of the Strait of Magellan.

The Strait Scoop

A strait is a narrow waterway betwee landmasses that connects two large bodies of water. The Florida Strait, between the Florida Keys and Cuba, carries the Gulf Stream current from the Gulf of Mexico to the Atlantic Ocean. The Strait of Gibraltar, betwee Spain and Morocco, connects the Mediterranean Sea to the Atlantic Ocean. The Bering Strait, between Russia and Alaska, connects the Pacif Ocean to the Arctic Ocean.

WHERE is the longest mountain range?

The Andes Mountains stretch 5,500 miles along the west side of South America from Venezuela to the southern tip of Chile. The world's second-highest mountain range (after Asia's Himalayas), the Andes have many peaks more than 19,000 feet high. Among them are Cotopaxi, the highest active volcano on Earth, and Aconcagua, at 22,834 feet, the highest mountain in the Western Hemisphere.

But there are more than high mountains in the Andes. In the north, there are dense rain forests on the slopes and in the valleys. In the Peruvian Andes, the Amazon River starts its 4,225-mile-long journey to the Atlantic Ocean. In the central Andes lies the Altiplano, a high plateau that is second in size only to the Tibetan plateau in Asia. The Andes are also home to grasslands, deserts, salt flats, and glaciers. Many of the glaciers are melting as Earth's climate warms.

People have lived in the Andes Mountains for about 12,000 years—and many native peoples still do. Quechua, which has been spoken for about 2,000 years, is an official language in Peru and Bolivia. Four countries have their capitals in the Andes: Bogotá, Colombia; Quito, Ecuador; La Paz and Sucre, Bolivia (yes, Bolivia has two capitals); and Santiago, Chile. La Paz, at 11,913 feet above sea level, and Quito, at 9,350 feet, are the two highest capital cities in the world.

Floating Villages

Straddling the border of Peru and Bolivia, Lake Titicaca is the largest freshwater lake in South America. It lies 12,500 feet above sea level on the Altiplano plateau in the Andes Mountains. The Uros people have lived on Lake Titicaca for more than 500 years. They build their homes on artificial islands they make out of totora reeds.

Closest to the Stars

Measured from sea level, Mount Everest, on the border of Nepal and China, is the highest mountain on Earth. But it's not the closest peak to the sun, moon, and stars. Why? Instead of being perfectly round like a ball, Earth has a bulge around its middle—and Mount Chimborazo in Ecuador sits squarely on top of it. Add to that its height of 20,700 feet, and Chimborazo tops out at about 1.25 miles closer to the stars than Mount Everest!

Road of Death

Bolivia's old North Yungas Road has claimed between 100 and 300 lives every year, so it's no surprise that it was nicknamed the Road of Death. Winding about 40 miles through the Andes Mountains, the road has no guardrails, even where steep cliffs rise up on one side and plunge down more than 1,500 feet on the other. Other hazards include fog, rain, waterfalls spilling into the road, and landslides.

Highest Peaks in the Andes

1. ACONCAGUA, ARGENTINA
   22,834 FEET

2. OJOS DEL SALADO, ARGENTINA–CHILE BORDER
   22,615 FEET

3. MONTE PISSIS, ARGENTINA
   22,287 FEET

4. CERRO BONETE, ARGENTINA
   22,175 FEET

5. TRES CRUCES, CHILE
   22,142 FEET

WHERE is the world's largest tropical rain forest?

Nearly everything about the Amazon rain forest is mind-boggling. It's about four times the size of Alaska and covers parts of eight countries (Peru, Bolivia, Ecuador, Colombia, Venezuela, Guyana, Suriname, and more than half of Brazil) as well as the territory of French Guiana. Parts of the forest get up to nine feet of rainfall per year. About half of that is produced by evaporation and water vapor given off by plants and trees. About 30 million species of plants and animals live in this hot, humid environment, while about 3,000 species of fish live in the forest's rivers.

The rain forest has four main layers. Harpy eagles fly above the *emergent layer,* where the tops of 200-foot-high trees poke up out of the *forest canopy.* Here, orchids and bromeliads grow among the tangled leaves and branches, and the vines of lianas (climbing plants) loop from tree to tree. Colorful macaws (large parrots) squawk and chatter in the trees, and the cries of howler monkeys can be heard for miles.

Very little sunlight filters through the canopy to the *understory* of young trees and shrubs. Below, the *forest floor* is dark and covered with leaves. Roaming these two lower layers are jaguars and 200-pound capybaras, the world's largest rodent. Swampy areas harbor crocodiles and 29-foot-long anaconda snakes. And among the thousands of creepy crawlers are giant stick insects, Goliath birdeater tarantulas, beetles that are half a foot long—and clouds of mosquitoes.

EMERGENT LAYER

CANOPY

UNDERSTORY

FLOOR

Poison dart frogs are tiny (less than 2 inches long) but their skin contains a deadly toxin.

Slow-moving sloths spend most of their time hanging upside down and resting.

Bromeliads are epiphytes (*eh*-puh-fites), or air plants. They grow in trees and get their nutrients from the air and rain.

Sunken Rain Forest

More than 300 million years ago, an earthquake dropped the level of the land beneath a swampy rain forest. Water and mud flooded in and buried it. Fast-forward to the present, when the fossilized floor of the forest was found. Where? In the ceiling of two coalmines in eastern Illinois in the U.S. Because the forest was buried so suddenly, much of it was preserved.

Hundreds of macaws flock to the clay banks of the Manu River in Peru's rain forest. They come to chow down on clay, which helps counteract the poisons found in some of the seeds that they eat.

WHERE did people first dance the tango?

Sailors, dockworkers, gauchos (cowboys), and other workers came from Europe, the Caribbean, Africa, and other South American countries, to find jobs in Buenos Aires, Argentina. Along with their skills, they brought their music with them. In the 1880s, they developed a new musical form and dance they called the tango.

At first, the middle and upper classes of Buenos Aires disapproved of the tango's close dancing. But when it reached Paris, France, in the early 1900s, the tango became a dance craze that spread to other European countries, the U.S.—and back to Buenos Aires, where it became popular with everyone.

Over the years, the tango has been featured in stage performances, movies, and plays. Today, dancers from all over the world visit Buenos Aires to compete in the Tango Dance World Cup and Festival held every August.

Maria Noel Sciuto from Uruguay and Cristian Sosa from Argentina won the 2012 Tango Dance World Cup in the stage-dancing category.

CAFÉ RICHE

TANGO
Dansé par
Jack
et sa Danseuse

Imp. GAILLAC-MONROCQ & C.3, Rue Sauer.

Maxine Brésilienne

Atelier Georges REDON. 63, Rue NOLLET.

Women dancers began wearing tango shoes like the ones in this 1914 poster for a tango show in Paris. Straps or laces up the front kept the shoes from falling off during the dance.

The Hully-Gully

Dance Crazed!

In the 1960s, early rock-and-roll singers and their bands created a rash of dance crazes with funny names, including the Twist, the Swim, the Mashed Potato, the Hully-Gully, the Loco-Motion, the Jerk, and the Pony.

WHERE was the first FIFA World Cup played?

On July 30, 1930, more than 80,000 people crowded into a brand-new stadium in Montevideo, Uruguay. They were there to watch the home team and Argentina compete for the first FIFA World Cup. Since its founding in 1904, FIFA—*Fédération Internationale de Football Association*, or the International Soccer Association—had wanted to stage a world championship, and the game was finally at hand.

Planning had begun in 1928. Italy, Netherlands, Spain, Sweden, and Uruguay were interested in hosting the match. FIFA chose Uruguay, which would celebrate 100 years of independence in 1930—and had offered to build a new stadium as well as pay travel expenses for the teams. Thirteen teams signed up to play, including the U.S., Mexico, seven South American countries, and four European countries.

Now the play-offs were over, and Argentina and Uruguay were about to face off in the final match. By halftime, Argentina was ahead 2–1. But in the second half, Uruguay scored three more goals to win the first World Cup 4–2.

An aerial view of the stadium in Montevideo, Uruguay, where the final game for the first FIFA World Cup was played.

Uruguay scores the winning goal in the 1930 FIFA World Cup final.

Soccer or Football?

Soccer was first called association football—*fútbol* in South America—and it still is just about everywhere but in the U.S. and Canada. Why soccer? Around 1889, the middle part of the word *association* somehow got shortened to *socca*—which later became soccer.

Living Legend

Many fans and experts think of Brazil's Edson Arantes do Nascimento—better known as Pelé—as the best soccer player of all time. During his first World Cup championship game in 1958, Pelé scored two goals, contributing to Brazil's 5–2 win over Sweden. And he was only 17 years old! Eleven years later, Pelé scored his 1,000th goal. He retired from the game in 1977.

WHERE can you find the world's largest natural mirror?

Covering an area of 4,086 square miles, the Salar de Uyuni is the largest salt flat in the world. The Salar lies more than 2 miles above sea level in the Altiplano plateau of southwest Bolivia. In the wet season, the salt is slow to absorb the rain. As a result, a shallow sheet of water covers the salt flat, turning it into a giant natural mirror.

The salt crust in the Salar is more than 30 feet deep and contains about 10 billion tons of salt. About 25,000 tons a year are piled into cone-shaped mounds that are trucked away for sale. Underneath the salt crust is slushy brine (salt-filled water) that contains lithium, which is used in batteries for electric cars, laptop computers, cell phones, and many other electronic devices.

Except for a few "islands" that rise up out of the salt, the Salar is so flat that NASA uses it to gauge the distance between its satellites and Earth. There is little animal or plant life except on these islands. The largest is Incahuasa Island, also called Fish Island because of its shape. Cactuses up to 40 feet high can be found there, along with wild dogs and rodents that look like rabbits except for their long tails.

If you visit the Salar de Uyuni, you can stay in a hotel built with salt blocks. Even the beds, tables, chairs, and other furniture are made out of salt!

Cactuses up to 40 feet high grow on the "islands" of Bolivia's salt flats.

Racing Flats

In the U.S., the hard, dry surface of the 45-square-mile Bonneville Salt Flats in Utah attracts racecar drivers from all over the world. Instead of racing against each other, drivers race against the clock to set land speed records. In 1970, Gary Gabelich set a world record when he drove his rocket-powered Blue Flame 622.4 miles per hour.

WHERE was a church built on a bridge?

The Church of Our Lady of Las Lajas ("flat rocks") is high in the Andes Mountains in southwest Colombia, near the border with Ecuador. The front of the church opens onto a bridge 165 feet above the rushing waters of the Guáitara River, and the back is set into the rock of the cliff face. Amid this rugged scenery, the Gothic-style church is a startling sight. Although it appears to have been there for hundreds of years, the church was begun in 1916 and finished 33 years later on the site of an earlier shrine.

The main altar of the church frames a section of flat rock adorned with the image of Mary holding the baby Jesus. Legend has it that a child discovered the painting in a cave in 1754 and a miracle occurred: The child suddenly spoke for the first time in her life. Word spread that the picture could perform miracles, and that's why a shrine was erected.

When the current church was built, scientists tested the image. They said they found no paint on the surface of the rock. Instead, the colors were part of the rock itself and extended deep into the wall. So who put the picture in the cave? How was it made? It's a mystery.

Marvelous Mud

The town of Djenné, Mali, in northwest Africa has another amazing structure built for religious purposes. The Great Mosque of Djenné was constructed from sun-dried mud bricks and is the largest mud-brick structure in the world. The mosque suffers damage from alternating spells of hot, dry weather and heavy rains. Every year, the townspeople have a festival when they get together to smooth and repair the mud walls.

Salt of the Earth

The Salt Cathedral of Zipaquirá, Colombia, lies 600 feet underground. It was carved out of an ancient rock-salt mine and is big enough to hold several thousand people.

Europe

The northern lights put on a dazzling show in Norway.

Home to the birthplace of Western civilization, Europe is the site of many cultural centers, including Athens, Greece; Paris, France; London, England; Berlin, Germany; Madrid, Spain; Rome, Italy; and Vienna, Austria. Here you'll find fairytale castles, the ruins of ancient temples, and magnificent cathedrals. Among the natural wonders of the second smallest continent are the fjords of Norway, the hot springs of Iceland, and rugged mountain ranges such as the Alps, the Caucasus, and the Pyrenees.

The Matterhorn in the Alps on the border of Switzerland and Italy

Germany's Neuschwanstein Castle, built in the late 1800s, was the model for Walt Disney's Magic Kingdom.

Reykjavík

0 mi   300 mi
km   300 km   600 km

IRELAND

ATLANTIC OCEAN

GUE
JER

BAY
BIS

Porto   Bilb

PORTUGAL

Lisbon   Madrid

SPAIN

Faro   Seville

Málaga
Gibraltar

MOROCCO

A F R I C A

WHERE were LEGO bricks invented?

In 1932, a carpenter named Ole Kirk Kristiansen started a company in Billund, Denmark, that made wood stepladders, ironing boards, and toys. He named the company LEGO, a word formed by combining the first two letters of *leg* and *godt*, the Danish words for "play well." Soon, Kristiansen was making only high-quality toys out of wood. After World War II, LEGO started producing plastic toys. In 1949, the company launched Automatic Binding Bricks, its first interlocking construction blocks.

In the 1950s, the name was changed to LEGO bricks, and the company came out with the LEGO System of Play, which included 28 sets and 8 vehicles. It also began selling the toys outside of Denmark for the first time. In 1958, LEGO received a patent for the modern bricks so famous today. The new bricks not only had studs on top, but tubes inside that lock onto the studs of other bricks and hold them securely together.

Today, the company produces billions of LEGO parts a year. They are sold all over the world. In fact, enough LEGO Bricks are sold every year to circle the world five times if laid end to end!

Workers show off some of the toys and other wood products produced by LEGO in 1932.

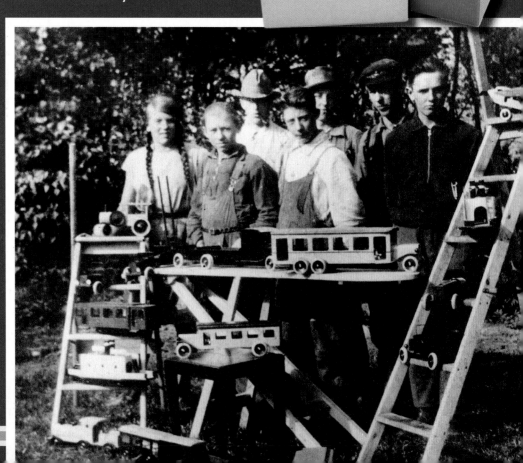

Play Value

New York City's Nathan Sawaya is proof that you can have fun and make a living at the same time. In 2004, he gave up his job as a lawyer to become a full-time artist—making sculptures out of regular LEGO bricks you can buy in any toy store. But Saway buys them by the thousands. In fact, he has about 1.5 million in his studio! Among his creations is a 20-foot-long *Tyrannosaurus rex* (left).

In 2012, the city of Prague, Czech Republic, captured the world record for the tallest tower created from LEGO bricks. It took a half-million bricks to build the 106.6–foot tower.

WHERE did the roller coaster get its start?

Imagine climbing up to a platform 50 to 70 feet high, then *whooshing* down a steep ice-covered ramp. If you're lucky, you're sitting on a slab of ice or a wooden sled with a rope to hang onto but nothing to steer with. At the bottom, there's only a bit of sand and maybe a couple of bumps to slow you down. That's what ice slides, or "ice mountains," in Russia were like about 400 years ago. And everyone loved them—even royalty! The 18th-century Russian empress Catherine the Great liked them so much, she even had her own built in the palace grounds.

The problem with ice slides was that they could only be enjoyed in the winter. So someone had the bright idea to run wheeled cars along a sloping track. Experts disagree on whether the first roller coasters were built in Russia or France, but by 1817, France had two of them. Both had cars with wheels that locked to the tracks. Their heritage is clear, however: The French call roller coasters "Russian mountains."

This watercolor painting shows the empress Catherine the Great (in sled, bottom right) visiting the Ice Mountain in St. Petersburg, Russia, in 1788.

Coney Island Thrills

The first roller coaster built for an amusement park opened in Coney Island, New York, on January 16, 1884. It was called the Switchback Railway, probably after a railroad in Pennsylvania that was built to haul coal but also became a thrill ride for tourists. The Cyclone, built on the site of the Switchback Railway, opened in 1927—and is still operating today. Its wood cars are pulled 85 feet up the wood tracks before plunging back down at 60 mph.

G-Force

Roller coasters work mainly by gravity. But now you don't have to climb to a platform at the top in order to get the ride of your life. You can get into a car, which is pulled up the first high hill by a motorized chain. A pause at the top—and *whoosh!*—down you go, often at speeds of more than 100 mph. Since they're going so fast, the coasters can get up the smaller hills on their own. Then down they go again, picking up enough speed to get up the next hill . . . and the next.

WHERE did an artist spend four years on his back painting a ceiling?

Actually, nowhere. Although a book and movie portray Michelangelo Buonarotti as lying on his back to paint the ceiling of the Sistine Chapel in Vatican City, it just wasn't so. He did, however, spend four years standing on ledges and platforms 65 feet high and bending his head back to paint. In a funny poem, Michelangelo described his discomfort: "My beard toward Heaven, I feel the back of my brain upon my neck . . . In front of me my skin is being stretched while it folds up behind and forms a knot."

Michelangelo used the fresco technique, applying paint to the plaster of the ceiling while it was still wet. Although he probably used assistants to make the plaster and grind and mix the colors, Michelangelo did all the painting. More than 400 life-size figures illustrate scenes from the Bible. Despite the pain Michelangelo suffered, he created a masterpiece that has astonished visitors for more than 500 years.

Mighty Small

Vatican City lies completely within the city of Rome, Italy. At less than a quarter of a square mile, the Vatican may be the world's smallest country, but it is the center of the world's largest Christian religion, Roman Catholicism.

In addition to being home to the pope, the head of the Catholic Church, the Vatican has its own newspaper, radio and television stations, websites, postal stamps, publishing company, libraries, and an observatory to study the stars. It even has its own army: the Swiss Guard, whose duty is to protect the pope as it has done for more than 500 years.

TOP 5

Smallest Countries in the World

1. VATICAN CITY	.17 SQ. MI.
2. MONACO	.77 SQ. MI.
3. NAURU	8.1 SQ. MI.
4. TUVALU	10 SQ. MI.
5. SAN MARINO	23.5 SQ. MI.

WHERE do people use boats instead of cars?

In Venice, Italy, no cars are allowed outside the one big parking lot at the edge of the city. Instead, people get around on *vaporetti,* the motorized bus-boats that travel its many canals. Or they wander through the narrow, winding streets and alleys on foot, crossing the canals on the city's 400-plus bridges.

How did such a city come to be? More than 1,500 years ago, raiders from northern Europe reached Italy. Under attack, some of the people fled the mainland for a group of small, sandy islands in the Venice lagoon. Over the years, they created a city. Because its 118 islands wouldn't hold much weight, Venice was built on platforms supported by millions of wood piles (posts) driven into the islands and the seabed.

Venice is one of the most beautiful cities in the world, and every day, about 60,000 tourists come to admire it. They hop a *vaporetto* and cruise the Grand Canal or take a boat ride to the nearby island of Murano, famous for its blown glass. Some enjoy a ride on a gondola, the traditional flat-bottomed boat steered by an oarsman standing in the back. And many simply sit outside in St. Mark's Square to eat and people-watch.

A *vaporetto* (bus–boat) on the Grand Canal

VE 7963

The Bridge of Sighs was given its name by Lord Byron, a British poet. Legend has it that convicted prisoners would sigh as they crossed the bridge to the prison and got their last glimpse of Venice.

High Water

High tides, full moons, and strong, warm winds that blow from Africa across the Mediterranean and Adriatic Seas sometimes combine to cause flooding in Venice. *Acqua alta* ("high water"), as the Venetians call it, has been happening for centuries. The good news is that it only takes place from October to December and the water goes down when the tide goes out. The bad news is that it's been happening more often, probably because of global warming.

Gondolas have been around for centuries, but now they are mostly used to give rides to tourists or for weddings and funerals.

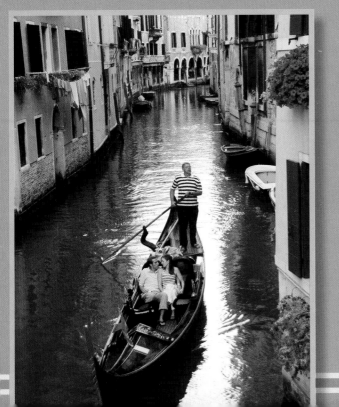

Saving Money on Gas

People in Venice get around on boats, but in the Netherlands, many people ride bicycles not only for fun and exercise but also to get places. Kids ride their bikes to school—where they have to pass a bicycle safety test—while their parents cycle to work or to the store. In Amsterdam, about half a million people ride their bikes to work. There are bike lanes throughout the city as well as bicycle traffic lights, road signs, and parking lots.

WHERE is the country with the cleanest energy?

In Iceland, people swim outside all year round, even in the coldest months when the average temperature is 28°F—not so bad for a place that's just barely south of the Arctic Circle. On the other hand, the average summer temperature is only 60°F, so swimming can be a challenge even then. Luckily for Icelanders, the island is a hotbed of volcanic activity, which means there are natural hot springs.

But all that volcanic activity has a more important benefit: It produces geothermal energy (heat from inside Earth). In Iceland, geothermal energy fills 87% of the nation's heat and hot water needs and 25% of its electricity needs. Geothermal energy is not only a clean energy source but also a renewable one.

What does that mean? Clean energy is generated without producing or releasing carbon dioxide into the air. Renewable energy is generated by the sun, wind, water, or volcanic activity. In Iceland, 75% of the electricity is produced by hydroelectric (water) power, a clean energy source. So not counting fuel for cars and other vehicles, nearly 81% of Iceland's energy comes from clean sources. That's more than any other country in the world.

Blowin' in the Wind

Wind turbines harness the power of the wind to produce electricity. Many countries, including China, the U.S., and Germany, are using more of this clean, renewable power source. Recently, the U.S. passed Germany in the amount of energy produced by wind power, and officials say it may get as much as 20% of its electricity from this source by 2030.

TOP 5
Countries with the Cleanest Energy

Here are the countries with the highest percentage of people using clean energy.

1.	Iceland	80.6%
2.	Sweden	46.2%
3.	France	45.6%
4.	Norway	43.2%
5.	Switzerland	40.9%

A side effect of one of Iceland's geothermal power plants is the Blue Lagoon, which formed when excess water flowed into a nearby lava field. Its milky aqua color comes from blue-green algae, rock, and natural chemicals in the land. Today, the Blue Lagoon is the site of a popular spa.

WHERE is the world's most visited art museum?

Every year, almost nine million people come from all over the world to visit the Louvre (*lou*-vruh) in Paris, France. When the first building went up more than 800 years ago, however, it wasn't a museum but a fortress. When the city grew up around it, the fortress, no longer used for defense, was transformed into a palace for the king.

In the 1600s, the royal family moved to a new palace just outside Paris. The old palace was then used for exhibits. Finally, on August 10, 1793, the Louvre opened as a museum. Admission was free. Artists could visit anytime, but the public was only allowed in on weekends. The works on display were mostly paintings from the collections of the king and other noble families. The Louvre has been growing ever since.

Today, the museum's collection includes about 380,000 works of art, with about 35,000 on display. Among the most famous are the *Law Code of Hammurabi, King of Babylon*; the *Winged Victory of Samothrace*; the *Venus de Milo*; and Leonardo da Vinci's *Mona Lisa*.

Works of Art from the Louvre

The Winged Victory of Samothrace once stood on the prow of a sculpture of a huge ship. It was carved into a rocky hilltop on the Greek island of Samothrace about 2,200 years ago.

The Mona Lisa—painted by Leonardo da Vinci in the early 16th century, is one of the most famous paintings in the world.

The Law Code of Hammurabi, King of Babylon, is nearly 4,000 years old—older than the laws set down in the Bible.

Unusual Museums

If you happen to be in England, you can visit the Dog Collar Museum, the Lawnmower Museum, and the Cumberland Pencil Museum. But England's not the only place with unusual museums. At the Museum of Questionable Medical Devices in Minnesota, you can see a machine that measures the bumps on your head to figure out your personality. The SPAM Museum in Austin, Minnesota, is all about the canned meat (not junk mail). And in California, the Burlingame Museum of PEZ features the world's largest PEZ dispenser (left), which is 7 feet 10 inches high.

In the 1980s, during the construction of a new main entrance to the Louvre, the remains of the 12th-century keep (fortified tower) and the 14th-century moat were uncovered.

WHERE did the largest invasion by sea take place?

On D-Day, June 6, 1944, more than 155,000 British, American, and Canadian armed forces stormed the beaches of Normandy in German-occupied France. World War II had begun in Europe in September 1939, when Nazi Germany invaded Poland, and Great Britain and France declared war on Germany. By the middle of 1940, Germany had invaded and occupied several other countries, including France, and Italy had joined the war on the German side. By 1944, Germany controlled most of mainland Europe.

But the Allies (the countries fighting against Germany, Italy, and Japan in the Pacific) had a daring plan. They were going to land a massive force on the coast of France in an effort to drive the Germans back. The obvious place to attack was the port of Calais, the point in France that is closest to England, just across the English Channel. But Calais was heavily fortified, so the Allies decided to land on the Cotentin Peninsula in Normandy.

At 6:30 on the morning of D-Day, more than 5,000 ships and landing craft carried thousands of Allied troops to five beaches along a 50-mile stretch of coast. Overhead, more than 10,000 aircraft provided air cover. By the end of June, the Allies had 850,000 men and 150,000 vehicles in Normandy, and by the end of August, they had driven the Germans out of France. Thanks in part to the D-Day invasion, the war in Europe would end in less than a year.

Gotcha!

Nazi Germany knew the Allies would probably attack them in northern France but not exactly where. The Allies wanted to keep it that way, so they decided to play a huge trick. They created a whole army of fake soldiers in southeastern England with fake bases and filled them with fake trucks, tanks, and other vehicles. They gave out fake information through newspapers, radio broadcasts, and spies. And it worked! The Germans were so sure the Allies were going to attack the port of Calais that they kept most of their forces there even after the Allies had landed in Normandy.

Speaking in Code

During World War II, the Allies were fighting Japan in the Pacific and needed a code that the Japanese couldn't break. The Navajo language is complicated and has no alphabet, so in 1942, 29 marines who were Navajos created a code. They used Navajo words for military terms, like *besh-lo,* which means "iron fish" and stood for submarine. The code, which had to be memorized by the Navajo code talkers, proved to be unbreakable, and they are credited with saving hundreds of thousands of lives.

WHERE is the biggest machine on Earth?

The Large Hadron Collider—LHC for short—runs in a 16 3/4-mile-long loop about 300 feet beneath the border of France and Switzerland. It weighs more than 37,000 tons. What the LHC does is send two beams of atomic particles called hadrons speeding around the loop. When the particles are going at almost the speed of light, the LHC lets them collide at four special places on the loop called detectors. So what's the point?

The big machine helps scientists find out what the universe—and everything in it—is made of. The energy created when the hadrons collide in the LHC is as powerful as the energy released just a tiny fraction of a second after the Big Bang. (That's the gigantic explosion that scientists think created the universe.) Every second, millions of collisions create thousands of new atomic particles that weren't there before. The tricky part is picking out the important ones.

It's the job of the detectors to track the new particles and the job of scientists working all over the world to figure out what they are and what they do. That's how scientists discovered the Higgs-boson, the particle that gives things mass—in other words, the reason there's matter in the universe and not just energy. Without it, there would be no stars, moons, planets—or people.

Vital Attraction

In 1964, the Scottish scientist Peter Higgs came up with a theory about how matter is formed by energy. He thought that the universe was filled with a field that contained a special kind of boson (an atomic particle that carries force). As fast-moving (energetic) particles passed through the field, they attracted these special bosons. And the clumping of bosons around the energetic particles slowed them down enough to create mass, which is necessary for matter to exist. In 2012, experiments in the Large Hadron Collider found that special boson—now called the Higgs-boson—proving Higgs was right.

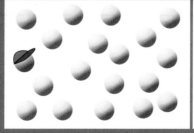

Imagine a bunch of Higgs-bosons in a box. A fast energetic particle (with cap) enters and starts across the box.

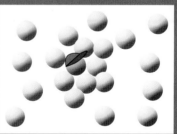

Some of the Higgs-bosons are attracted to the energetic particle and gather around it, slowing it down— and creating mass.

WHERE can you find the "World of the Ice Giants"?

Every year, about 200,000 people visit the world's largest ice cave in Austria.

The "World of the Ice Giants" is the name of a 25-mile-long cave system high in the mountains above Werfen, Austria. The name comes from the thick ice that forms inside the first 3,500 feet, creating the world's largest ice cave.

The maze of caves started to form about 100 million years ago as the limestone mountain began to erode. The reason ice can form is because the crevices (cracks) that connect different levels of the cave allow air to circulate. In winter, freezing cold air streams into the cave and settles into the lower areas. In spring, when melting snow and ice seep down into these areas, the water freezes. Because the cave is so cold even in the summer, the ice never completely melts. Instead, it just gets thicker and forms ever-growing stalactites and stalagmites.

The cave wasn't explored until 1879 because the people who lived nearby thought it was the entrance to hell—even though it was freezing cold and lined with ice. After that, nobody paid much attention to it until 1912, when more explorers ventured inside. Within just a few years, it had become a tourist attraction.

Up and Down

Stalactites hang down from the ceilings of caves and stalagmites grow up from the floors. In limestone caves, they're made of a mineral called calcite. When rain seeps through limestone, it dissolves the mineral and carries it along. When the water reaches the ceiling of a cave, the calcite starts to solidify and, over time, it forms a stalactite. A stalagmite forms when dissolved calcite reaches the floor, often under a stalactite. Sometimes the two join together and become a column.

Taking Giant Steps

Ireland's volcanoes are extinct, but that wasn't the case 60 million years ago. And the north coast of Northern Ireland has the evidence to prove it. There, volcanic activity created 40,000 hexagonal (six-sided) columns that stretch from the land into the sea. The columns are made of basalt, a type of volcanic rock. The area is called the Giant's Causeway. According to legend, the giant Finn McCool built the causeway so he could cross the channel to Scotland and visit his lady friend.

Asia

More than 35 million people live in Tokyo, Japan, the world's largest city.

Everything about Asia is huge! It's the largest continent and home to more than four billion people. That's three times as many people as there are in Africa, which has the second largest population. About 2.5 billion people live in China and India alone. In Asia you'll find the highest mountain range, the longest railroad, the busiest subway system, the deepest freshwater lake, and the oldest surviving civilization on Earth.

In 2012, a new study set the length of the Great Wall of China at more than 13,000 miles, over twice as long as earlier measurements.

The giant panda lives in southwest China, where it survives on the leaves, shoots, and stems of the bamboo plant.

ARCTIC OCEAN

United States

Bering Sea

Chersky

NORWAY
SWEDEN
FINLAND

Tiksi

Verkhoyansk

Magadan

Kamchatka Peninsula

Petropavlovsk-Kamchatskiy

ESTONIA

DENMARK

GERMANY

RUSSIA
LATVIA
LITHUANIA

POLAND
BELARUS

Yakutsk

R U S S I A

Sea of Okhotsk

Sakhalin

CZECH REPUBLIC

E U R O P E
SLOVENIA
HUNGARY
UKRAINE

Khanty-Mansiysk

S I B E R I A

YUGOSLAVIA
ROMANIA
MOLDOVA

KOSOVO
BULGARIA

Yekaterinburg

Chelyabinsk

Khabarovsk

Istanbul
Black Sea

Magnitogorsk

Imeni Gastello
Astana

Tomsk
Krasnoyarsk

Novosibirsk
Novokuznetsk

Irkutsk

Sapporo

TURKEY
Ankara
GEORGIA
Tbilisi

Caspian Sea

KAZAKHSTAN

Omsk

Harbin

Vladivostok

JAPAN

Adana
ARMENIA
Yerevan

Aral Sea
Tyuratam

Qaraghandy (Karaganda)

Ulaanbaatar

Changchun

Shenyang
NORTH KOREA

Sapporo

CYPRUS
Nicosia
Baku
AZERBAIJAN

Nukus
UZBEKISTAN

Bishkek
Almaty

MONGOLIA
Gobi

Hohhot
Beijing

Pyongyang
SOUTH KOREA
Seoul
Pusan

Tokyo

LEBANON
Beirut
SYRIA
Damascus

TURKMENISTAN

Tashkent
Samarkand
Fergana

Urumqi

Taiyuan
Tianjin

Jinan

Kyoto
Nagoya
Kobe Osaka
Hiroshima

PACIFIC OCEAN

ISRAEL
Tel Aviv
Amman
Baghdad

Ashgabat
Dushanbe
TAJIKISTAN

KYRGYZSTAN

Fukuoka
Nagasaki

Jerusalem
JORDAN
IRAQ

Mashhad

Lanzhou

Xi'an

Qingdao

Tabuk
Basra
Kermanshah

Herat

CHINA

Hefei
Shanghai

Kuwait City
IRAN
Esfahan

Kabul
Islamabad

Lhasa

Chengdu
Chongqing

Wuhan

Red Sea
KUWAIT
Shiraz
Kerman

Quetta

Srinagar
Claimed by India

Nana

BAHRAIN
Manama
Doha
Abu Dhabi

Riyadh
QATAR

Faisalabad
Multan

Delhi

NEPAL
Kathmandu
Thimphu
BHUTAN

Fuzhou

Xiamen

Taipei

TAIWAN

Jidda
Mecca

Muscat

Karachi

Kanpur

Liuzhou
Guangzhou

Kao-hsiung

SAUDI ARABIA
OMAN
Arabian Sea

PAKISTAN

INDIA

BANGLADESH
Dhaka

Nanning
Macau
Hong Kong (special admin. region)

Sanaa

Nagpur

Kolkata (Calcutta)

Chittagong
Mandalay

Hanoi

YEMEN

UNITED ARAB EMIRATES

Mumbai (Bombay)
Pune

Hyderabad

MYANMAR (BURMA)
Nay Pyi Taw

LAOS
Vientiane

Luzon

Baguio

Quezon City

ERITREA

Taizz
Al Mukalla

Bay of Bengal

Chiang Mai

Da Nang

Manila

DJIBOUTI
Aden

0 mi   500 mi   1,000 mi

Bangalore

THAILAND
Bangkok

VIETNAM

PHILIPPINES

Cebu

ETHIOPIA

0 km 500 km 1,000 km

Chennai (Madras)

CAMBODIA
Phnom Penh

Ho Chi Minh City

Davao

Cochin
Madurai

Colombo
Jaffna
SRI LANKA

SOMALIA

INDIAN OCEAN

Bandar Seri Begawan

Ipoh

Manado

MALDIVES
Male

Phuket
Songkhla

Kota Kinabalu
BRUNEI

Jayapura

Sorong

Irian Jaya

M A L A Y S I A
Medan
Kuching
Borneo

Samarinda
Palu
Celebes

New Guinea

Pakanbaru
Kuala Lumpur
SINGAPORE
Singapore

Pontianak

Sumatra
Palembang

Banjarmasin

I N D O N E S I A

Ujungpandang

Every year, millions of people travel to Mecca, Saudia Arabia, to visit the Ka'aba, the holiest building in Islam.

WHERE was the Silk Road?

The Silk Road was a communications highway long before computers ever existed. It wasn't just one road but a number of trade routes that stretched across Asia from the Mediterranean Sea to Chang'an (now Xian) in eastern China, with branches to India. Camel caravans going east carried wool, gold, glass, and other goods from Europe and Africa. In China and India, the merchants traded their goods for silks, jade, spices, and other things to sell at home. Along the way, cities became centers where people also traded ideas, customs, beliefs, music, and artistic styles.

Across central Asia, the Silk Road wound thousands of miles over harsh deserts and high mountains. Between cities, travelers stopped at oases to rest. After the tenth century, they could stay at caravansaries (care-uh-*van*-suh-reez). These large stone buildings served as inns, where people and their animals could rest and be safe from bandits.

A picture of a caravan on the Silk Road appears in an atlas dated 1385.

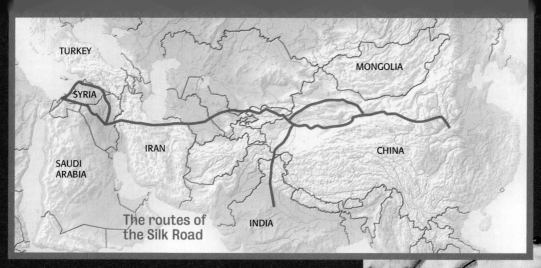

The routes of the Silk Road

On the Road

Marco Polo was only 17 years old when he set off from Venice, Italy, in 1271 with his father and uncle. They traveled on the Silk Road to China, where the emperor Kublai Khan welcomed them. A few years after returning home in 1295, Polo wrote *The Travels of Marco Polo*. Almost 200 years later, the book inspired Christopher Columbus to look for a western sea route to Asia.

Long Time Gone

In 1325, when Ibn Battuta was 21 years old, he left home—and didn't return for almost 30 years. He traveled from Morocco all the way to China. Among the places he visited were Spain, North and East Africa, the Arabian Peninsula, western Russia, and Indonesia. When he finally got back home, Battuta had traveled nearly 75,000 miles.

WHERE can you find fairy chimneys and underground cities?

Cappadocia in central Turkey is a magical landscape of fairy chimneys, cones, and rippled valleys as well as rock houses and ancient underground settlements. They are all carved out of tuff. This soft rock was formed from thick layers of ash left behind by volcanoes millions of years ago. Over a long time, heavy rains and melting snow eroded the tuff, sculpting it into the strange shapes that attract tourists from all over the world.

About 3,500 years ago, people began making their homes out of the rock. Over the centuries, they built more than 35 underground cities. The cities provided shelter as well as a place for people to hide from their enemies. The largest known city is Kaymakli, which has eight floors, staircases, ventilation shafts, and almost 100 tunnels. Scientists think more than 3,000 people may have lived there, and its underground rooms and tunnels are still used as stables and storage areas. The deepest city is Derinkuyu, which goes down more than 275 feet.

The "caps" on the fairy chimneys in Cappadocia are made of harder stone than the worn-away rock just below them.

Some of Cappadocia's ancient rock homes have eroded into fantastic shapes.

City of Stone

The city of Petra in southwest Jordan was half built and half carved out of the red sandstone cliffs of a narrow gorge about 2,000 years ago. Once a busy city at the crossroads of a trade route connecting Arabia with China, Petra was home to about 20,000 people. Today, it is mostly empty except for tourists and their guides.

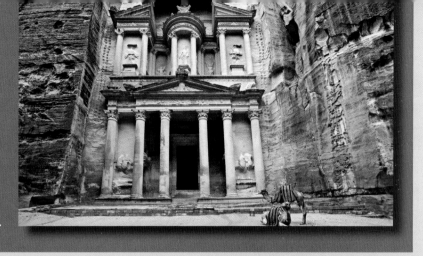

These eroded cliffs in Cappadocia look like the whipped-cream peaks on an ice-cream sundae.

Rooms and tunnels in the underground city of Kaymakli in Cappadocia

Mountain Command Center

There's a modern-day underground city in the U.S. In 1961, a military command center was blasted out of the granite 2,000 feet under Cheyenne Mountain in Colorado. Built to withstand a nuclear bomb, its 15 buildings are protected by two 25-ton blast doors, air filters, and water and fuel reservoirs. Today, about 600 people work there. One of their jobs is to look for unidentified aircraft in the skies over the U.S. and Canada.

CHEYENNE MOUNTAIN COMPLEX

WHERE was language written down for the first time?

It seems that writing was invented to help keep track of property and to record business deals. At least, that's what it was used for in the oldest writing samples found so far. They were discovered in southern Mesopotamia (present-day Iraq) in the ruins of an ancient city called Uruk. The language is called Sumerian, and the samples date back more than 5,000 years.

The earliest writing was in word pictures called pictograms. Each object had its own pictogram. Over time, the word pictures developed into wedge-shaped signs that are called cuneiform (kyu-*nee*-uh-form) writing. Sharpened reed "pens" were pushed into soft clay tablets, which were hardened by baking in a kiln, or oven. After a while, the signs began to stand for ideas and sounds as well as objects. That's when people started to write down the names of gods and kings and record the different things they did.

The Egyptians invented hieroglyphs at about the same time the Sumerians invented cuneiform writing. They had as many as 800 symbols. Some of them stood for sounds and some stood for objects or ideas. These symbols took a lot of time to write, so the Egyptians came up with simpler symbols for everyday work called hieratic (hi-uh-*ra*-tik) writing. Later, they came up with even simpler symbols called demotic (dih-*mah*-tik) writing.

Cracking the Code

After the Egyptians stopped using hieroglyphs, their meanings were forgotten for more than a thousand years. In 1799, a black stone slab now called the Rosetta Stone was found. On it were three different kinds of writing: hieroglyphic, demotic, and ancient Greek, which people could still read. A language expert cracked the code to reading both kinds of ancient writing.

The writing on the stone plaque at left says that the figure is Enannatum, the ruler of a city–state in Mesopotamia. The clay tablets above are an accounting of donkeys and carts (top) and a list of farmers and the land they received as wages.

WHERE do people drive brightly decorated trucks?

The roads of Pakistan are filled with trucks covered with bright colors and decorations. The owner usually pays for the work, but the driver or the artist often decides how the truck will be decorated. The work is all done by hand and can take a month or more to complete.

Although each truck is unique, there's a pattern to the decorations. The front often has a religious theme, with a *taj*, or wooden prow, built over the cab. Side panels are painted with landscapes and animals. The back panel is usually a large portrait surrounded by flowers or geometric patterns. Calligraphy (kuh-*lih*-gruh-fee), a kind of writing, includes prayers, poetry, and even funny sayings.

In a truck-painting shop, there are people to build the *taj* and attach the panels. Other workers decorate metal mud flaps and fasten jingling metal balls or disks around the bottom of the truck. Woodworkers carve door panels for the cab. And, of course, artists create the paintings and mosaics, which are sometimes made of reflective tape. Inside, the cabs are decorated with tiny mirrors, plastic flowers, and embroidered seat cushions and window flaps.

Art on the Go

Decorated vehicles aren't unique to Pakistan. In the 1960s, a group of writers who called themselves the Merry Pranksters traveled across the U.S. in a brightly painted school bus (above). During the 1960s and '70s, hippies decorated their Volkswagen Beetles and buses, and singers like Janis Joplin and John Lennon (below) painted their cars in colorful patterns. Since then, decorated cars, or "art cars," have become so popular, there are festivals, museums, and websites devoted to them.

WHERE did a subcontinent collide

About 50 million years ago, India drifted north through an ancient sea and crashed into Asia. How did it happen? Earth's crust and upper mantle are cracked into pieces that fit together like a jigsaw puzzle. The puzzle pieces are called plates, and they move around on the superhot melted rock of the lower mantle. Ocean crust is denser and heavier than the crust under a landmass. So when an ocean plate collides with a continental plate, the ocean plate slides underneath.

As the Indian plate neared Asia, its leading edge of ocean crust slid under the Eurasian plate. Tibet's crust buckled and was pushed upward along with scraped-off parts of the seafloor. The Indian plate kept moving until finally, India rammed into Asia. The collision of the two landmasses

with Asia?

caused the earth to crumple, fold, crack, and twist as it was pushed upward—to become the high peaks of the Himalaya Mountains, the tallest on Earth.

Today, scientists say India is still pushing up against Asia, and the Himalayas are still getting higher. How fast are they growing? Less than half an inch a year.

On Top of the World

The tallest mountain in the world is Mount Everest in the Himalayas on the border of Tibet (part of China) and Nepal. How high is it? China says it's 29,017 feet. Nepal says 29,029 feet, but that's including the snowcap, not just the rock. In 1999, another measurement by American scientists using GPS put the height at 29,035 feet. But no matter which measurement you choose to believe, Mount Everest still comes out on top.

First to the Top

On May 29, 1953, the first mountaineers reached the top of Mount Everest. They were Sir Edmund Hillary of New Zealand and Tenzing Norgay of Nepal. The men

were two of a dozen climbers in a team that included 35 guides and 350 porters. After two other climbers tried and failed to reach the summit, Hillary and Norgay set off—and made it all the way up.

WHERE do more than 1 billion people live?

More than 1.34 billion people live in China. Although the country is slightly smaller than the U.S., it has about four times the number of people. In 1979, China passed a law to slow down its growth: each married couple was allowed to have only one child. Partly because of this law, experts believe that within the next 15 years, India will have more people than China. Today, India is in second place with 1.2 billion people.

China is the oldest surviving civilization in the world. Its written history goes back more than 3,500 years. The Chinese were the first to make silk, paper, printed books, and gunpowder. They were also the first to use paper money. Among their inventions are the wheelbarrow, kite, compass, and seismograph (*size-muh-graf*), a device used to detect earthquakes.

Muslim armies from Iran conquered India in the early 1500s and founded the Mughal Empire. It lasted for 400 years, and is famous for its art and architecture. After the mid 1800s, India was a colony of England until 1947, when it gained its independence. Today, it is the world's largest democracy.

Downtown Calcutta, India

Shanghai, China's largest city

India's Taj Mahal is one of the most beautiful buildings in the world. It was erected by the emperor Shah Jahan as a tomb for his favorite wife.

Jobs to Go

In the last 10 to 15 years, many American and European businesses have been hiring companies in India to do computer processing and routine office work, like customer service. That's because the Indian people have good English-language skills and were willing to do the work for less money. Today, higher-paying and more interesting jobs, like testing car safety and designing computer programs, are also being done in India.

WHERE is the world's busiest subway system?

If you don't like crowded spaces and you're in Tokyo, Japan, stay away from the subways, especially at rush hour. Every year, more than three billion people crowd into the city's subways. In fact, there are so many people trying to get on during rush hours that the subway companies hire *oshiya*, or "pushers."

Wearing uniforms and white gloves, the pushers shove as many people as they can into the subway cars while making sure the doors can still close. That can sometimes be twice the number of people the cars were designed to hold. Think sardines in a can and then double it! Can you imagine what it's like trying to get out at your station if you're packed into the middle of one of these overcrowded subway cars?

Busiest Subways

Here is the yearly ridership for the world's busiest subways.

1. TOKYO, JAPAN: 3.1 BILLION

2. SEOUL, KOREA: 2.51 BILLION

3. BEIJING, CHINA: 2.46 BILLION

4. MOSCOW, RUSSIA: 2.39 BILLION

5. SHANGHAI, CHINA: 2.28 BILLION

A pusher packs the last person into a subway car in Tokyo, Japan.

Golden Oldie

The world's oldest subway system is in England. The London Underground—also called the Tube—celebrated its 150th birthday on January 9, 2013. The first line was a little less than four miles long. Today, the Underground has more than 250 miles of track and 275 stations. More than one billion passengers ride the Tube every year.

WHERE is the longest railroad in

The Trans-Siberian Railway is more than 5,770 miles long. It winds across Russia from Moscow to Vladivostok, a port city on the Sea of Japan. Along the way, the train crosses the Ural Mountains, where Europe meets Asia, and seven time zones. It takes eight days to make the trip, with one overnight stop.

Passengers can buy a ticket for a first-, second-, or third-class sleeping car. A first-class compartment has two sleeping berths and second class has four. Third-class cars have a long walkway down the middle with berths like bunk beds stacked up on both sides. Each car has just one bathroom for everyone. *Providnitsas*, or train attendants, collect tickets, keep the cars clean, and deliver meals.

Some travelers change trains at Tayshet, about halfway across Russia, and take the northern branch, called the Baikal Amur Mainline. After crossing seven mountain ranges and traveling through areas that get as cold as −76°F in winter, the branch line reaches the Sea of Japan at Sovetskaya Gavan.

The Trans-Siberian train leaves from Moscow's Yaroslavsky station (above) and arrives in Vladivostok (right).

the world?

The Trans-Siberian Railway

____ main branch

____ northern branch

RUSSIA

Moscow

Tayshet

Lake Baikal

KAZAKHSTAN

MONGOLIA

CHINA

Sovetskaya Gavan

Vladivostok

Sea of Japan

Way Deep

With a depth of more than 5,250 feet, Siberia's Lake Baikal is the deepest lake in the world. It's also one of the biggest, with as much water as all five of North America's Great Lakes put together. The water is so clear, you can see down as far as 130 feet. More than 740 of the animals that live in or around Lake Baikal are unique to the area. The most famous are the Baikal seals, the world's only freshwater species.

WHERE were the oldest maps found?

Not every expert agrees on which map is the oldest—or even whether an early picture map is really a map or just a picture. The oldest maps everyone agrees on were found in southern Mesopotamia (present-day Iraq). One map found in the ruins of Ga-Sur dates back to either 2500 B.C. or 3800 B.C., depending on which expert is writing about it. The next oldest are pieces of small clay tablets from about 1500 B.C. that map the city of Nippur as well as the fields and canals around it.

The oldest world map is from the same area in Iraq and dates back to 700–500 B.C. It pictures the ancient city of Babylon in the center. Circling the city is a waterway that represents the ocean. Triangles around the ocean's edge stand for different areas the Babylonians called "islands." Writing describes each area and notes the distance between them.

Mapping the Stars

The oldest known star map was found in a cave near Dunhuang, a town along the Silk Road in China. Twelve separate maps were drawn on a long roll of paper and date back to the mid 7th century A.D. They accurately map the entire night sky and show 1,339 stars and 257 constellations. Some experts believe the maps may have been copied from an even older star chart.

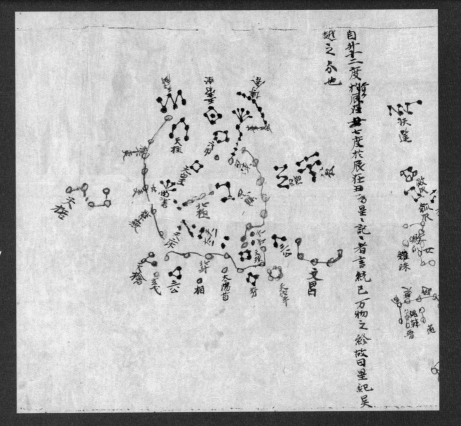

Lost and Found

Today, it's hard to get lost if you have a cell phone or handheld GPS device. Powered by computers and satellites, the Global Positioning System can place you within about 10 feet of wherever you are. GPS is used by hikers, drivers, pilots, sailors—anyone who needs to keep track of where they are and find their way from one place to another. And, of course, it's used in map making.

WHERE do more than 17,500 islands make up a country?

The Republic of Indonesia is the world's largest group of islands. The bigger islands include Sumatra, Java, Sulawesi, about three-quarters of Borneo (also called Kalimantan), and half of New Guinea. Among the smaller islands are Bali, which is famous for its beautiful white-sand beaches, and the Moluccas, which were once called the Spice Islands.

Indonesia also holds a few other world records. The country has about 76 active volcanoes, more than anywhere else on Earth. It is home to the Komodo dragon, the largest lizard, as well as the world's largest flower. The *Rafflesia arnoldii* flower can be up to three feet across and weigh as much as 15 pounds. The Titan arum is even bigger—up to 12 feet high and 170 pounds—but its blossom is not one but thousands of tiny flowers. The flowers of both plants smell like rotting meat.

Shadow Play

In Indonesia, *wayang kulit*, or shadow puppets, are very popular. The puppets are traditionally made by hand. After a pattern is traced onto stiff leather, it is cut out and painted, and the arms and hands are attached separately. Sticks fastened to the back allow the puppeteer to move the puppets around behind a white screen. A light behind the puppets projects their shadows onto the screen, and the puppeteer acts as the storyteller.

From left:
The Titan arum is also called the corpse flower because it smells so bad.

The Komodo dragon can grow up to 10 feet long and weigh more than 300 pounds.

The *Rafflesia arnoldii* plant is a parasite: it attaches itself to another plant and steals its water and nutrients.

Mountain of a Thousand Statues

The largest Buddhist temple in the world is in Java, Indonesia. Sometimes called the mountain of a thousand statues, Borobudur was built more than 1,200 years ago. The rectangular base is formed of five stepped platforms. Next come three round platforms studded with stupas (*stoo*-puhz), or shrines, that each contained a statue of the Buddha. At the top is a single large shrine. The temple stands for a person's journey from the material to the spiritual world.

Africa

Where can you visit the world's largest hot desert, fly over a 4,000-mile-long valley where the continent is breaking apart, sail along one of the world's longest rivers, find more unique animal species than anywhere else—and view the birthplace of humankind? Africa! Earth's second largest continent is also home to the second largest tropical rain forest. (South America's Amazon rain forest is number one.) Africa is also number two in population, after Asia. A billion-plus people live in 53 countries and speak more than 2,000 different languages.

Hippopotamuses are among the most dangerous animals in Africa. They're big, they're fast, they bite, and they're quick to attack.

Cheetahs can reach a speed of 40 miles per hour in just three strides—that's faster than some cars—and have a top speed of 70 miles per hour, faster than any other animal.

In 2012, the population of Lagos, Nigeria, grew to 20.5 million people, making it the largest city in Africa.

ATLANTIC OCEAN

EUROPE

FRANCE SWITZERLAND AUSTRIA HUNGARY MOLDOVA

SLOVENIA

BOSNIA AND SERBIA

Corsica ITALY HERZEGOVINA MONTENEGRO KOSOVO BULGARIA

SPAIN

BLACK SEA

GEORGIA

ARMENIA

PORTUGAL

Majorca Sardinia ALBANIA MACEDONIA ASIA

Madeira Islands

Tangier

Algiers Oran Constantine Tunis

Sicily GREECE

Crete

TURKEY

Casablanca Rabat

Fes

Marrakech Erfoud

MALTA

MEDITERRANEAN SEA

CYPRUS

LEBANON SYRIA

IRAN

Tripoli Banghazi

Alexandria ISRAEL

IRAQ

Canary Islands

Laayoune

MOROCCO

TUNISIA

Cairo Suez

JORDAN

BAHRAIN

QATAR

WESTERN

SAHARA

(Occupied

by Morocco)

ALGERIA

S A H A R A

LIBYA

EGYPT

Luxor

Aswan

RED SEA

SAUDI ARABIA

Al Jawf

MAURITANIA

MALI

NIGER

Port Sudan

Nouakchott

Timbuktu

Agadez

Khartoum

ERITREA

Asmara

YEMEN

Dakar

SENEGAL

Niger R.

Bamako

Niamey

Zinder

CHAD

N'Djamena

SUDAN

DJIBOUTI

Djibouti

Banjul

BURKINA

FASO

Addis Ababa

Harer

Hargeysa

THE

GAMBIA

Bissau

GUINEA

Ouagadougou

Kano

NIGERIA

Gore

ETHIOPIA

Conakry

Gaoua

BENIN

Abuja

SOMALIA

GUINEA-

BISSAU

Freetown

COTE

D'IVOIRE

GHANA

Ibadan

Lagos

Benue R.

CENTRAL AFRICAN

REPUBLIC

Juba

SOUTH SUDAN

SIERRA

LEONE

Monrovia

LIBERIA

Yamoussoukro

TOGO

Porto-Novo

CAMEROON

Yaoundé

Bangui

UGANDA

KENYA

Abidjan

Accra

Loma

Douala

Kampala

Mogadishu

Malabo

Congo R.

RWANDA

Lake

Victoria

Nairobi

Equator

EQUATORIAL GUINEA

SAO TOME

AND PRINCIPE

Libreville

REPUBLIC OF THE

CONGO

Kigali

Bukavu

BURUNDI

Mombasa

Annobón

(EQUATORIAL GUINEA)

GABON

Brazzaville

Bujumbura

Kigoma

Lake

Tanganyika

Dodoma

Zanzibar

Dar es Salaam

INDIAN

OCEAN

Pointe-Noire

Kinshasa

Kananga

TANZANIA

ATLANTIC

OCEAN

Luanda

DEMOCRATIC

REPUBLIC OF

THE CONGO

Lubumbashi

Lake

Nyasa

Moroni

COMOROS

ANGOLA

Kitwe

MALAWI

Lilongwe

Nacala

Namibe

Lubango

Lusaka

Blantyre

MOZAMBIQUE

Antananarivo

ZAMBIA

Harare

Beira

MADAGASCAR

NAMIBIA

ZIMBABWE

Mozambique Channel

BOTSWANA

Walvis Bay

Windhoek

Gaborone

Pretoria

Maputo

Johannesburg

Mbabane

SWAZILAND

LESOTHO

Bloemfontein

Maseru

Durban

SOUTH

AFRICA

Cape Town

Port Elizabeth

0 mi   500 mi   1,000 mi

0 km   500 km   1,000 km

WHERE is the largest desert in the world?

The Sahara Desert stretches across northern Africa from the Atlantic Ocean to the Red Sea, covering an area almost as big as the United States. Most of the Sahara consists of broad plains covered with stones and gravel, but there are also barren mountains. And sand, of course. In some places, strong winds sweep across the desert and blow the sand into huge dunes up to 1,000 feet high and hundreds of miles long. These areas of sand dunes are called *ergs*, from the Arabic meaning "sand sea."

Although the Sahara gets very little rainfall—in some places, only a half-inch per year—there is water in aquifers (*ak*-wuh-furs). These are underground layers of rock that allow water to flow through. Fertile areas called oases spring up in low places where the water is at the surface. Here, plants such as date palms and citrus can grow, and there is enough water to support people and livestock.

Shippers of the Desert

Before modern trucks, there was only one way to move goods around the Sahara Desert: camels. Camels can go for a long time with little water, and their broad feet keep them from sinking into the desert sands. The camel caravans were run by the Tuareg, a group of semi-nomadic tribes. Some Tuareg still operate camel caravans.

World's Largest Deserts

If you counted polar deserts, the Antarctic and Arctic would hold the number 1 and 2 spots. (The areas shown below are approximate.)

1. SAHARA DESERT, NORTH AFRICA
   3.3 MILLION SQUARE MILES

2. ARABIAN DESERT, SOUTHWEST ASIA (ARABIAN PENINSULA)
   900,000 SQUARE MILES

3. GOBI DESERT, CENTRAL ASIA
   500,000 SQUARE MILES

4. KALAHARI DESERT, SOUTHERN AFRICA
   360,000 SQUARE MILES

5. PATAGONIAN DESERT, ARGENTINA
   260,000 SQUARE MILES

Sandstorms can create a wall of sand nearly a mile high, and even blow sand right out of Africa and across the Atlantic Ocean to the Americas!

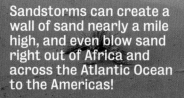

The roots of palm trees tap underground water to survive.

WHERE are the most pyramids?

Say the word *pyramid* and most people think of Egypt. But although Egypt has the biggest pyramids, it doesn't have the most. In fact, there are more than twice as many—about 220—pyramids in present-day Sudan, Egypt's southern neighbor. Many of Sudan's pyramids are in Meroe, which was once the capital of the Kingdom of Kush (also known as Nubia).

Where & When

Ancient pyramids or pyramid-shaped temples are found in many places around the world.

2667–2575 B.C.
Stepped Pyramid of Zoser (Egypt)

2550 B.C.
Great Pyramid at Giza (Egypt)

2100 B.C.
Ziggurat of Ur (Iraq)

260 B.C.–350 A.D.
Pyramids of Kush (Sudan)

The pyramids in Sudan are smaller than those in Egypt and have steeper sides. Today, most of the pyramids in Meroe look like their tops were knocked off—and they were. In the 19th century, an Italian treasure hunter named Giuseppe Ferlini broke into the pyramids, looking for gold. Out of all the pyramids he wrecked, Ferlini found gold in only one, and he sold it to European museums.

Welcome to Earth

Ziggurats were built in the ancient land of Mesopotamia, which stretched from southern Turkey through Syria and into Iraq. They were huge stone structures with stepped sides. Ziggurats were meant to be landing places for the gods when they came down to Earth.

The Biggest of Them All

Egypt's Great Pyramid was built by the pharaoh Khufu. It is made of more than 2 million blocks of stone—and each of the stones weighs 2.5 tons. That's a lot of weight to move around, especially when all you have to move it with are barges and heavy sleds pulled by people or oxen!

200 B.C.–A.D. 800
Great Pyramid of Cholula (Mexico)

12 B.C.
Pyramid of Cestius (Italy)

ca. A.D. 150–250
Pyramids of Teotihuacan (Mexico)

ca. A.D. 700–800
Step pyramids of Tikal (Guatemala)

WHERE does the Nile River begin?

When the British explorer John Speke came upon Africa's Lake Victoria in 1858 and saw all that water, he thought he'd found the source of the Nile River. But it turns out that it's not so easy to trace the source of a river. Major rivers have other rivers feeding into them, and it can be hard to figure out exactly which tributary leads to the source.

The Nile River begins where the White Nile and the Blue Nile meet in Sudan. The White Nile is the longer of the two rivers and starts in Lake Victoria. The lake, however, also has tributaries, and the largest one is the Kagera River.

In 2005 a group of explorers set out to travel the Nile from the Mediterranean Sea to its ultimate source. After reaching Lake Victoria, they followed the Kagera using GPS equipment. In March 2006, they found a muddy spring in a forest in southern Rwanda and declared that it was the true source of the Nile.

The explorers measured the length of the Nile River at 4,175 miles, which may make it the second longest river in the world. In 2007, researchers from Brazil traced the source of the Amazon River, and estimated its length at 4,225 miles—50 miles longer than the Nile. Which group is right? Time will tell.

Strong currents swirl the waters of the White Nile River in Uganda.

Cairo, on the Nile River, is the largest city in Egypt.

Most of Egypt is desert, except for the land that borders the Nile River. There, deposits of sediments during flood times enrich the soil, allowing it to support both crops and cattle. Today, 95% of Egypt's people live along the banks of the Nile, even though it makes up only 5% of the land.

River Dams

Sometimes the flooding of the Nile River in Egypt was so bad that it washed away entire crops. To control the flooding, engineers built two dams across the Nile. The Aswan Low Dam opened in 1902, and the Aswan High Dam opened in 1970. These dams allowed Egypt to protect its crops not only in times of flood but also in times of drought, by storing water in the lakes formed by the dams.

Aswan High Dam

Major Move

The opening of the Aswan High Dam would result in a huge reservoir called Lake Nasser. But there was one problem: the new lake would cover Abu Simbel, two huge temples carved out of the solid rock of a cliff more than 3,000 years ago. The solution? Move the temples! The entire complex was cut into blocks weighing up to 30 tons each, moved to higher ground, and put back together.

WHERE is the Sahel?

Sahel comes from the Arabic word for "shore." In Africa, the Sahel is the 3,000-mile-long strip of land that separates the dry Sahara to the north from the wooded savannas (grasslands) to the south. Although the Sahel averages 4 to 20 inches of rainfall a year, it has periods of drought when it gets little or no rain at all. These droughts can last for many years, causing crops to die, food shortages, and even war over who controls what water there is. It's not only people who compete with each other for water. Plant life is often the main source of water for desert animals. The tiny Senegal gerbil, the most common mammal in the Sahel, gobbles up as much as 10% of the area's plants. Larger animals, like elephants and giraffes, sometimes raid farmers' crops for food.

Many of the Fulani people of the western Sahel still move with their herds in search of grazing land and water. The more animals they have, the richer they are.

Animals in Danger

As the supply of water in the Sahel drops, farmers and herders do whatever they can to water their crops and their herds. Who loses out? The wild animals, many of them large grazing animals that are already endangered because of overhunting. And as the numbers of grazing animals decline, so do the numbers of their predators, such as the lion, the wild dog, and the cheetah, who are losing an important food source.

Red-fronted gazelle

Cliffside

Many of the Dogon people, who are mainly farmers, live in Mali. The Dogon are famous for the carved masks that the men wear in religious ceremonies. One of their beliefs is that about 3,000 years ago, they were visited by beings from the star Sirius. Every 60 years, young men take part in a ceremony that marks the appearance of Sirius between two mountains.

WHERE is Africa splitting apart?

Red Sea

Gulf of Aden

Ethiopian Rift

East African Rift

Eastern Branch

Lake Victoria

Mt. Kilimanjaro

Lake Tanganyika

Western Branch

?

A Samburu warrior looks out at the Great Rift Valley in Kenya.

It's going on right now in the Great Rift Valley, one of the few places on Earth where you can see a continent breaking apart. A rift is a fracture, or crack, in Earth's crust. Rifts are caused by hot, thick melted rock called magma rising up underground. As the rift widens, a valley forms between the two sides. And as the rift gets wider, the valley sinks deeper.

The rift system in eastern Africa formed more than 25 million years ago. It runs almost 4,000 miles south from the Red Sea and the Gulf of Aden to Mozambique. Millions of years from now, the easternmost parts of Africa will break off and form an island.

The Red Sea and many of Africa's Great Lakes were created when deep rifts filled with water. At a depth of about 4,800 feet, Lake Tanganyika is the deepest lake in Africa. The rift zone also includes volcanoes. In Tanzania, Mount Kilimanjaro, Africa's highest mountain, is a volcano, though it hasn't erupted for about 10,000 years.

A Little Bit of Africa in Your Tank

If you have ever kept an aquarium at home, you may have kept some species of African freshwater fish. More than 500 species of cichlids (*sik*-luhdz), such as the electric yellow lab and jewel cichlid, are found in Africa's Great Lakes. They are very colorful and breed easily, which is why they are such popular aquarium fish.

Think Pink

Lake Natron in Tanzania is a shallow lake fed by mineral-rich hot springs. Among the few creatures that can live in its hot, salty water are *Spirulina*. These bacteria have red pigments that give color to the lake—and to thousands of Lesser Flamingos that flock there during nesting season.

WHERE did scientists find the oldest human ancestors?

Many of the bones and other fossil remains of ancient human ancestors were discovered at dig sites in the Great Rift Valley in Ethiopia and Tanzania. It makes sense when you think about it. If man and apes share common ancestors, the natural place to look for their fossil remains would be in Africa, where most of the great apes come from.

Tanzania's Olduvai Gorge is the most famous of the Rift Valley dig sites. After more than 20 years of digging, scientists Louis and Mary Leakey made their first discovery. In 1959, they found a skull that belonged to a stage between apes and people. It was .25–1.75 million years old. Since then, other discoveries have been made in the Rift Valley, including the remains of a 4.2 million-year-old species identified in 1994 by Meave Leakey, Louis and Mary Leakey's daughter-in-law.

The .25–1.75-million-year-old skull found in the Olduvai Gorge in 1959

Louis and Mary Leakey examine fossils from an early human ancestor.

The Great Migration

Where did the first early people go when they left Africa? Scientists are using DNA and fossil evidence to figure it out. Here's what they've pieced together so far:

Number of Years Ago	Location
80,000–60,000	Mid-East and India
By 45,000	Indonesia, Papua New Guinea, Australia
By 40,000	Eastern Europe/ Mediterranean coast
By 35,000	Western Europe
By 15,000	North America and later, South America

Out of Eden Walk

It took humans thousands of years to populate the world, starting in Africa and finally reaching South America. Can you imagine trying to walk that distance? In January 2013, American journalist Paul Salopek began a journey of 22,000 miles, from Ethiopia in Africa, through Asia to North and South America, all the way to the southern tip of Chile. His purpose: to highlight issues facing our planet by telling the stories of the people he meets along the way.

WHERE is the Skeleton Coast?

A shipwreck on the Skeleton Coast lies half-buried in sand.

The Skeleton Coast used to be the name for the entire coastline of Namibia, the driest country in Africa south of the Sahara Desert. Back when the world depended on whale oil for fuel, the name referred to all the whale bones left by the sailors who hunted them. In modern times, the name is a nod to all the shipwrecks that litter the beaches.

Today, Skeleton Coast refers mainly to the national park in the northern part of Namibia.

The park is so remote that it has only a few access roads. Most visitors come on flying safaris, and there is plenty to see: huge, windswept dunes give way to dry salt flats, rugged canyons of reddish-orange volcanic rock, and strange clay formations. And of course, there is the fog that covers everything with an air of mystery. The fog, along with strong surf and a rocky coast, has caused many shipwrecks, but it also brings life-giving moisture to plants and animals.

Sand-Surfing Elephants

It may not seem possible, but the world's biggest land animals—elephants—also live in the Namib Desert. Over the years, these elephants have adapted to their dry environment. They have slightly smaller bodies and bigger feet than other African elephants, which make it easier for them to walk on the sands. (They've even been filmed surfing down a dune to get to water.) The desert elephants have learned to walk long distances to find water and know how to dig for water underground.

The cold ocean currents carry lots of nutrients, including plankton and krill by the ton. It also brings plenty of fish for the thousands of hungry Cape fur seals that breed on the Skeleton Coast.

The elephant's foot plant is native to the Namib Desert. Its round bottom stem can grow up to about 3 feet in diameter.

The fog-basking beetle drinks the moisture that collects on its body.

WHERE do lemurs live?

The island of Madagascar has the world's largest number of unique animal species. In fact, about 90% of Madagascar's plants and animals are found there and nowhere else. Madagascar split off from mainland Africa about 165 million years ago. That has given the island's plants and animals plenty of time to develop differently from their original ancestors.

Probably the most famous island creature is the lemur, a cousin of modern-day monkeys. Lemurs are more like prehistoric primates than they are like modern monkeys. Scientists think they may provide clues on how primates—including humans—might have evolved.

There are 93 known species of lemur on Madagascar. But new discoveries are being made all the time. A 2011 report from the World Wildlife Fund said that more than 600 new plants and animals were discovered there in just 10 years.

A lemur takes it easy on a branch in the forest.

Clouds gather over the Isalo Mountains in Madagascar.

Madagascar is home to the world's smallest primate, the mouse lemur.

Home Destruction

Many of Madagascar's unique species are losing their forest homes to slash-and-burn agriculture. Farmers cut and burn trees to create fields for their crops. It can work on a small scale if the fields are later left unplanted long enough for the trees to regrow. But if there are too many fields and the same fields are planted year after year, the result is forest loss, erosion, and poor soil.

WHERE do poachers hunt black rhinos for their horns?

By the end of the 1960s, there were about 70,000 African black rhinos in the wild. Then poachers, or illegal hunters, went after the rhinos for their horns, which were used in folk medicines and to make objects such as knife handles. In 1993, there were fewer than 2,500 black rhinos. After they were declared a protected species, the rhinos started to make a comeback. But the process is slow because the females only give birth to one calf every few years.

Today, the market for rhino horns is greater than ever, and poaching is once again on the rise. From the mid-1990s to 2005, poachers in South Africa killed about 14 or 15 black rhinos a year. Every year since, the number has gotten higher. In the last three years, more than 1,000 black rhinos have been killed there.

In 2013, there were only about 4,800 black rhinos left in the wild. Most of them are in South Africa and Namibia, with small numbers in Kenya, Zimbabwe, Tanzania, and a few other countries. Rangers in national parks and private reserves are working hard to stop the poachers and save the rhinos.

Planned Removal

Some people have had veterinarians cut off rhinos' horns to keep them from being hunted. Then the animals are safe from poachers for the couple of years it takes for the horns to grow back. Some ranchers who keep herds of rhino say that safely harvesting rhino horns and selling them legally might prevent poaching in the future.

There are about 20,000 white rhinos. Most of them live in protected areas or private game reserves.

WHERE was the world's biggest diamond found?

Weighing in at 3,106.75 carats—or 1.37 pounds—the Cullinan diamond is the biggest uncut diamond found to date. It was discovered in a South African diamond mine in 1905. The story goes that someone spotted the rock glinting in the wall of the mine, dug it out, and took it to the main office. The clerks didn't believe it was a diamond and threw it out! Luckily, it was retrieved. The stone was not only a real diamond but one of unusually fine color and quality.

In 1907, the uncut diamond was mailed to King Edward VII of England for his 66th birthday. It took eight months to cut, grind, and polish the huge stone, which became nine large diamonds and 96 smaller ones.

The two biggest stones cut from the Cullinan diamond are part of the British Crown Jewels. The largest diamond, known as the Star of Africa, is at the top of the Sovereign's Scepter. The next largest, the Second Star of Africa, was set into the Imperial State Crown, which is worn by the monarch for important events.

Queen Elizabeth II wearing the Imperial State Crown

Hard Stuff

Diamonds are the hardest crystals there are—in fact, the word diamond comes from *adamas*, a Greek word that means "indestructible." The best diamonds are used to make beautiful jewelry. Most diamonds, however, are mined for industrial uses such as drilling, cutting, and polishing.

Different kinds of industrial diamonds

Carbon Crystals

Diamonds are made of carbon, one of the most common elements on Earth. What makes diamonds special is how they became crystals hundreds of millions of years ago. The superhot magma (thick liquid rock) below Earth's crust is under extreme pressure. When the heat and pressure were just right, carbon in the magma about 100 miles underground formed crystals. When the magma shot up to the surface in powerful volcanic eruptions, the crystals rode up with it. Most diamonds are found in the hardened volcanic pipes the magma traveled through. Others are found in rivers, washed there over time.

Diamond-bearing gravel

The largest diamond cut from the Cullinan on display (left) and as set in the Sovereign's Scepter (right)

TOP 5 World's Biggest Uncut White Diamonds

1. CULLINAN, 3,106.75 CARATS

2. EXCELSIOR, 997.5 CARATS

3. STAR OF SIERRA LEONE, 968.9 CARATS

4. GREAT MOGUL, 807.85 CARATS

5. MILLENNIUM STAR, 777 CARATS

WHERE can you get a coffin that looks like an animal, an airplane, a pineapple, or a bottle?

For the Ga people of southern Ghana and Togo in West Africa, a funeral has always been a celebration. It honors the life of the departed loved one and is believed to give him or her a good start in the afterlife. Then in the mid-1900s, a new tradition began: the fantasy coffin.

The story goes that a woodworker named Ata Owoo created a wonderful eagle-shaped chair for a chief to be carried around in. When another chief and cocoa farmer saw it, naturally he wanted a chair of his own, but in the shape of a cocoa pod. When he died before it could be finished, he was buried in it. That gave Owoo's apprentice the idea to build an airplane-shaped coffin for his grandmother because she had always wanted to ride in an airplane but never got the chance.

Since then, fantasy coffins have grown in popularity even though the cost—starting at about $500—may be equal to a year's wages for an average Ghanaian. The design of a fantasy coffin is drawn from the dead person's life. It could reflect his or her job, hobby, status, likes, even hopes or wishes. There have been coffins shaped like land and sea creatures, cars and trucks, cell phones, Coke bottles— almost anything you can think of.

A man opens a soda (top right)—but in this case, it's a coffin in the shape of a Coke bottle. Also shown are fantasy coffins shaped like an eagle (above) and a fish (below).

The Art of Recycling

In 1999, the Ghanaian-born sculptor El Anatsui picked up a garbage bag from the side of the road. Inside were thousands of bottle tops. He took the bag back to his studio in Nsukka, Nigeria, and started experimenting. The result? Tapestry-like wall hangings made from the cut and straightened metal tops fastened together with copper wire. His sculptures are both beautiful works of art and a statement on the waste people make.

Australia

Australia is the world's smallest continent and sixth largest country. Much of Australia is desert, so most of its people live in cities along the southeast coast. Because it is relatively far from other continents, Australia is home to some unusual animals, including kangaroos, koalas, and the world's only egg-laying mammals as well as the top five most poisonous animals on Earth. Oceania includes New Zealand, Papua New Guinea, and 10,000 other islands in the Pacific Ocean.

More than 30 million kangaroos live in Australia—that's about 8 million more kangaroos than people!

At more than 1,100 feet high and almost 6 miles around, Australia's Uluru (also known as Ayers Rock) is the biggest rock in the world.

and Oceania

ASIA

CHINA

JAPAN

TAIWAN

Tropic of Cancer

PHILIPPINE SEA

VIETNAM

CAMBODIA

PHILIPPINES

NORTHERN MARIANA ISLANDS
Saipan ★ (U.S.)
★ Agana ★ Guam (U.S.)

Wake Island (U.S.)

Johnston Atoll (U.S.)

Honolulu
Hilo
Hawaii (U.S.)

PACIFIC OCEAN

BRUNEI

MALAYSIA

SINGAPORE

Borneo

Celebes

Yap Islands
PALAU
Koror

Caroline Islands
MICRONESIA
⊕ Palikir

MARSHALL ISLANDS
⊕ Majuro

Kingman Reef (U.S.)
Palmyra Atoll (U.S.)

INDONESIA

Sumatra

Java

Dili

EAST TIMOR

Irian Jaya

New Guinea

Wewak

PAPUA NEW GUINEA

Port Moresby

⊕ Tarawa

KIRIBATI

Howland Island (U.S.)
Baker Island (U.S.)

Jarvis Island (U.S.)

Equator

★ Yaren District
NAURU

Gilbert Islands

Phoenix Islands

Line Islands

Marquesas Islands

Island

Ashmore and Cartier Islands (Australia)

Timor Sea
Darwin

Gulf of Carpentaria

Great Barrier Reef (Australia)

Coral Sea Islands (Australia)

Honiara ⊕
Guadalcanal

SOLOMON ISLANDS

Funafuti ⊕
TUVALU

TOKELAU (New Zealand)
Mata-Utu ★

WALLIS AND FUTUNA (France)

SAMOA
Apia ⊕

Pago Pago
AMERICAN SAMOA

COOK ISLANDS (New Zealand)

Society Islands

Papeete
Tahiti

Tuamotu Archipelago

INDIAN OCEAN

CORAL SEA

VANUATU
⊕ Port-Vila

⊕ Suva
FIJI

TONGA
Nuku'alofa ⊕

Alofi
NIUE (New Zealand)

Avarua ★

FRENCH POLYNESIA (France)

Derby

Cairns

Townsville

Mackay

Rockhampton Gladstone

NEW CALEDONIA (France)
Noumea

Kermadec Islands (New Zealand)

Adamstown ★

PITCAIRN ISLANDS (U.K.)

Tropic of Capricorn

AUSTRALIA

Alice Springs

Brisbane

Norfork Island (Australia)
Kingston (Australia)

Geraldton

Broken Hill

Sydney

Lord Howe Island (Australia)

NEW ZEALAND

Auckland

Kalgoorlie

Whyalla

Canberra

Perth

Adelaide

Esperance

Bunbury

Melbourne

Hastings
✪ Wellington
Christchurch

Chatham Islands

International Date Line

TASMAN SEA

Hobart

Dunedin
Invercargill

Tasmania

Stewart Island

0 mi   500 mi   1,000 mi

0 km   1,000 km

Platypuses may have bills, webbed feet, and lay eggs, but they are mammals, not ducks.

WHERE is the world's purest air?

If you find yourself in Tasmania, an island to the south of Australia, be sure to take a deep breath. It has the world's purest air, especially on the northwest side of the island. There, strong winds called the roaring forties blow air up from the Southern Ocean around Antarctica, where there is no air pollution. Because of Earth's rotation, the northerly flow of the winds is pulled sideways and hits Tasmania from the west, bringing cold, wet weather. There's not much land along the way to slow the winds, which can gust up to 124 mph.

The air brought in by the roaring forties is about as pure as you can get on Earth. There is even a research station on the northwest tip of Tasmania where scientists collect air samples and compare the air to other places around the world. They measure the main types of air pollution: greenhouse gases, like the carbon dioxide released by coal and other fossil fuels, and tiny particles of pollutants such as soot.

Cattle graze peacefully beneath a giant wind-power turbine in breezy northwest Tasmania.

Devils Down Under

On the Australian island of Tasmania, creatures called Tasmanian devils are in danger of dying out from a strange, fast-growing cancer. The animals that develop the mouth tumors usually die within six months. Worse, the cancer can be spread. And it happens quickly because the animals fight a lot and often bite each other. The good news is a few devils have become resistant to the cancer. In addition, scientists have released a small number of healthy animals on a nearby island. The hope is that the distance will protect these devils from the cancer.

Wet and Wild

The roaring forties winds drop so much rain in northwest Tasmania that it has created a special cool-weather rain forest. Many animals there have adapted to the cold and wet. None of the local snake species lay eggs. Instead, the babies are born live so they can stay warm for as long as possible.

WHERE is the longest fence in the world?

Australia's Dingo Barrier Fence twists and turns its way across more than 3,300 miles of Australia. The fence protects southeastern Australia from dingoes, or wild dogs.

When European settlers began to arrive in Australia, they brought along animals like rabbits and sheep. To the dingoes, these animals were a great new food source. No one minded that dingoes killed rabbits because there were so many of them. In fact, fences were built to try to keep the rabbits from spreading throughout the country. But killing sheep *was* a problem because people raised them for money.

The government tried to help by putting a bounty on dingoes: paying people to kill them. In 1948, the government suggested building the Dingo Barrier Fence. The wire mesh barrier is six feet high and extends another foot underground. It does a pretty good job of keeping out the dingoes, but it requires constant upkeep. And not everyone is happy about the fence. Some people think it should be torn down. Without dingoes around, the numbers of rats, foxes, and other imported animals that eat or compete with native animals explode. Where there are dingoes, those animals are kept in check and the native plants and animals have a better chance to survive.

Darwin

Cairns

Alice Springs

A U S T R A L I A

Brisbane

Perth

Adelaide

Sydney

Canberra

Melbourne

Hobart

____ Dingo Barrier Fence

Ships of the Australian Outback?

Camels were brought to Australia as working animals in the 1800s because much of the country is dry and camels can go for a long time with little water. When trucks replaced them, the camels were freed. Now there are more wild camels in Australia than anywhere else. Like other imported species, the camels compete with native animals for food and water. They can also kill plants and trees by eating all their leaves. This becomes a real problem when a dust storm kicks up and there's not enough plant life left to hold the soil in place.

Invasion of the Melaleuca

An alien species is threatening to take over Florida's Everglades and endangering the native plants. It's the melaleuca tree, a native of Australia. It grows fast and high, and just one full-grown tree can produce up to 100 million seeds. Without animals or pests to feed on it, the melaleuca took over as much as 20% of the undeveloped land in southern Florida. Since 1997, however, two Australian bugs have been set loose and are chowing down on the melaleuca trees, which are their favorite food. Luckily, the bugs aren't interested in American plants.

WHERE can you find the world's most poisonous snake?

It's a good thing that the inland taipan snake is so hard to find. This is one snake you just don't want to bump into. The inland taipan has such strong venom, or poison, that one drop can kill 100 people—or 250,000 mice. Another name for the inland taipan is "fierce snake." That's because of its venom, not its personality.

This shy reptile lives in the middle of Australia. Taipans, which feed mainly on hard-to-kill desert rats, have developed super-powerful venom. The venom works in several ways. First it makes your blood keep clotting, which knocks out your organs. Other toxins destroy your nerve endings so you can't move. Then, after your clotting factor (the stuff in your blood that helps form clots) is used up, you can't stop bleeding. The good news is that there is a very good antivenin (a serum that counteracts venom), and no human deaths by inland taipan snakebite have been recorded.

Which came first, the venom or the snake?

For a long time, experts thought that snakes came first, and then some of the snakes developed venom. But recent evidence has proven that a very early reptile developed venom—and that reptile evolved into two different lines, snakes and lizards. Some lizards, like the Komodo dragon, make venom. Even lizards that don't make venom still have the equipment to do so. The same goes for constricting snakes that squeeze their prey to death.

A worker in a laboratory gets ready to extract venom from a rattlesnake.

Most Venomous Animals

Would you believe all five live in or around Australia? Even the world's only venomous mammal, the platypus, lives there!

1. BOX JELLY
. . . .
2. STONEFISH
. . . .
3. BLUE–RINGED OCTOPUS
. . . .
4. INLAND TAIPAN
. . . .
5. FUNNEL–WEB SPIDER

One Scary Spider

Australia is home to the Sydney funnel-web spider, the world's most venomous spider. The male's bite is much more dangerous than the female's, which is unusual in the world of spiders. Funnel-web venom fires up the nervous system so that it goes on overload. Primates (people included) are very sensitive to funnel-web venom, but it doesn't have much effect on other mammals, like dogs and cats. It works really well on insects, though. That's the funnel-web's food of choice.

WHERE is the "Land of the Long White Cloud"?

Paragliding—jumping off a mountainside harnessed to a parachute-like canopy— is a popular sport in Queenstown, New Zealand.

At three times the weight of a mouse, New Zealand's giant weta is one big bug!

Aotearoa is New Zealand by another name. It means "Land of the Long White Cloud" in the language of the Maori people, whose ancestors first settled the islands. Made up of two main islands—North Island and South Island—and lots of small ones, New Zealand has many volcanoes, including some that are still active.

The volcanic activity produces hot springs that cover the mountains and forests of North Island in heavy mists. That's what the earliest settlers saw when they first arrived about A.D. 1250 from smaller islands to the east. The descendants of those settlers, the Maori, became a society of warrior tribes. In the 1600 and 1700s, Europeans arrived and took over their land. But the Maori held onto their culture. And in the 1990s, the government began returning the land. Today, Maori is one of the country's official languages.

South Island is colder than North Island and fewer people live there. It is famous for the spectacular beauty of the mountains, glaciers, and fjords in the Southern Alps.

Love That Smell!

Birds spend a lot of time preening (taking care of) their feathers. They also produce oil that makes their feathers waterproof. It turns out that the oil made by New Zealand birds is pretty stinky. When people arrived, they brought cats, rats, and other predators that were attracted by the smell. Since then, about 40 bird species have disappeared. Others, like the flightless kakapo parrot (left) and kiwi, are endangered.

WHERE are more than 800 native languages spoken?

Humans first sailed from southeastern Asia and Indonesia to the island of New Guinea about 50,000 years ago. There, they found dense tropical jungles and tall, craggy mountains. This rugged terrain divided the settlers so completely that more than 800 different tribal cultures developed, each with its own language.

Today, the eastern half of the island is the small country of Papua New Guinea and the western half is part of Indonesia. Many people who live in the most remote areas of the island are moving to larger towns and leaving traditional customs and tribal life behind. As a result, many of those 800-plus languages have fewer than 1,000 people who speak them. In fact, some of the languages have no living speakers at all.

The official languages of modern Papua New Guinea are Tok Pisin, English, and Hiri Motu. Both Tok Pisin and Hiri Motu combine parts of different languages. Tok Pisin, which formed over time from English and other local languages, is the most popular.

Here are just 335 of the languages actively spoken in Papua New Guinea:

Abu	Aribwaung	Beli	Buna	Fanamaket	Hahon	Kandas	Kominimung
Agi	Aruek	Berinomo	Bungain	Fembe	Haigwai	Kanggape	Kopar
Aighon	Aruop	Biage	Burui	Finongan	Hakö	Kaninuwa	Korak
Aiklep	Asaro'o	Biem	Chambri	Fiwaga	Hewa	Kap	Koro
Aiome	Asas	Bilbil	Changriwa	Forak	Heyo	Kapin	Koromira
Akolet	Auwe	Binahari	Daantani'	Gaina	Humene	Kapriman	Kove
Akrukay	Avau	Bipi	Dambi	Gal	Idi	Kare	Kumalu
Akukem	Awar	Bisis	Danaru	Galeya	Ikobi	Karnai	Kumukio
Amaimon	Awara	Bitur	Degenan	Ganglau	Imonda	Kasua	Kunja
Amal	Awtuw	Biwat	Dera	Gants	Inapang	Kayan	Laeko-Libuat
Ambrak	Awun	Biyom	Dia	Garus	Ipiko	Keak	Langam
Ambul	Ayi	Blafe	Dibiyaso	Gende	Isabi	Kele	Lawunuia
Amio-Gelimi	Baibai	Bo	Dima	Ginuman	Isaka	Keoru-Ahia	Leipon
Amol	Baimak	Bogaya	Doghoro	Gitua	Isebe	Kesawai	Lemio
Anam	Baluan-Pam	Bongu	Domu	Gnau	Jilim	Kibiri	Lenkau
Anamgura	Baramu	Bosmun	Domung	Gobasi	Juwal	Kinalakna	Lilau
Andai	Bariji	Bragat	Duau	Goodenough	Kairak	Kis	Loniu
Andarum	Barikewa	Brem	Elepi	Gorakor	Kairiru	Kiunum	Lou
Andra-Hus	Bau	Breri	Elkei	Gumalu	Kaki Ae	Kobol	Lungalunga
Angoram	Bauwaki	Bulu	Elu	Guntai	Kala	Koiari	Lusi
Anor	Bebeli	Bun	Ere	Gusan	Kalou	Koiwat	Ma

Up from the Mud

Some of Papua New Guinea's tribal people keep their traditions alive by sharing them with tourists. One such group is the Asaro Mudmen. The story goes that a rival tribe chased the Asaro into a muddy river. That night, the mud-covered villagers tried to sneak away. The enemy saw them and thinking they were ghosts, ran away. So the Asaro decided to use the look to scare enemies. Today, photos of the Mudmen have found their way into advertising and pop culture.

When In Doubt, Spit It Out

In 1989, Jack Dumbacher was taking part in a bird study in Papua New Guinea. As he was removing a songbird called a hooded pitohui (pit-ah-*hoo*-ee) from a net, it bit him. The cut stung so he stuck his finger in his mouth. When his mouth began to tingle and go numb, he got scared and tried not to swallow. The feeling went away in a few hours, but the same thing soon happened to another researcher. Dumbacher decided to find out what was going on. It turns out that pithouis carry a powerful poison—the same kind carried by poison dart frogs—and it comes from the small beetles they eat.

Ma Manda	Moikodi	Neko	Oune	Ronji	Tainae	Utu	Wogeo
Makayam	Mokerang	Neme	Owenia	Saep	Tangga	Uyajitaya	Wom
Malas	Mondropolon	Nen	Oya'oya	Sam	Tanguat	Valman	Womo
Male	Mongol	Nend	Pagi	Sarasira	Tapei	Vanimo	Wutung
Mali	Monumbo	Nete	Pahi	Sengo	Tauya	Wadaginam	Yaben
Malol	Morawa	Ngala	Pal	Setaman	Tiang	Wa'ema	Yabong
Mamusi	Morigi	Niksek	Panim	Sewa Bay	Titan	Wagawaga	Yagomi
Manem	Mouwase	Nimi	Pano	Sialum	Tomoip	Wagi	Yahang
Mapena	Mubami	Nimoa	Papitalai	Sihan	Torau	Wahgi	Yaleba
Maramba	Munit	Ningil	Parawen	Sileibi	Torricelli	Walio	Yamap
Marangis	Muratayak	Niwer Mil	Pare	Siliput	Tulu-Bohuai	Wamas	Yangulam
Maria	Murupi	Nomane	Pasi	Simbali	Tumieo	Wampur	Yangum Mon
Matepi	Musak	Nomu	Penchal	Simeku	Tuwari	Wanambre	Yaul
Matukar	Musar	Nuk	Ponam	Sinagen	Ufim	Wanap	Yekora
Medebur	Nabi	Nukna	Ramopa	Sinsauru	Ulau-Suain	Wára	Yerakai
Mehek	Nakame	Nukumanu	Rapoisi	Sori-Harengan	Umeda	Waruna	Yil
Mekmek	Nakwi	Nukuria	Rapting	Sowanda	Uneapa	Wasembo	Yis
Meramera	Nama	Odiai	Rawo	Suganga	Urapmin	Watiwa	Yoidik
Migabac	Nambo	One	Rempi	Sukurum	Urigina	Watut	Yout Wam
Migum	Namo	Ontenu	Rerau	Sumau	Urimo	Waube	Zenag
Minigir	Nanubae	Opao	Romkun	Tabriak	Utarmbung	Wogamusin	

WHERE were the first "bungee jumpers"?

Every April, on Pentecost Island in Vanuatu, an island country in the South Pacific, boys and men climb up a rickety tower made of brush and branches, tie vines to their ankles, and dive off. It's a ritual called *naghol*, or land-diving.

The ritual is meant to bless the yam harvest, and the only way that can happen is if the diver's hair brushes the ground. Because the vines aren't elastic, they have to be cut just the right length. If the vines are too short, there's no blessing—and the jumper could swing into the tower and smash it. If the vines are too long, the jumper could dive to his death. A difference of four inches is all it takes. The elders who cut the vines don't measure them. They know where to cut based on years of experience.

For boys, taking part in land-diving means they are growing up. They are allowed to start at age five or six. They dive off lower platforms, working their way higher as they get older. The top of the tower is about 100 feet high. When a boy makes his first dive, his mother watches from the ground while holding her son's favorite childhood item. After the dive, the item is thrown away, meaning that the diver is no longer a child.

Power Walk

In Australia, young aborigines (native people) do a walkabout. That means they have to survive on their own in the desert for six months. While there, they follow the songlines (paths) of their ancestors and celebrate their heroic deeds.

The Big Bounce

An adventurer from New Zealand named AJ Hackett was inspired by Vanuatu's land-diving ritual in the 1980s. Can you guess what he invented? The bungee cord. In 1987, Hackett snuck up the Eiffel Tower in Paris and camped there overnight. Then he launched himself off the tower with his stretchy bungee cord attached to his ankles. He was arrested (and released) a few minutes later, and a new extreme sport was born.

Each year, thousands of people around the world enjoy the thrill of bungee-jumping.

WHERE did the word tattoo come from?

In 1769, the English explorer Captain James Cook wrote about the people of Tahiti in his journal. He said that men and women on this South Pacific island "paint their Bodys, Tattow, as it is called in their Language." Today, of course, *tattow* is tattoo.

Tatau means "to tap again and again." It makes sense when you know how a traditional tattoo is applied. The tattoo artists use a tool with a narrow wood handle. At one end, a small piece of turtle shell is fastened at a 90-degree angle. Attached to the shell is a kind of sharp-toothed comb carved from the tusk of a boar, or wild pig. The artist dips the comb in ink and then uses a second stick to tap the teeth of the comb into the skin. This kind of tattooing takes two people: one to stretch the skin tight while the other creates the tattoo. The process can take hours or even days.

The people of the South Pacific had no written language, so they used artwork to tell folk tales and legends and to show family background and rank in society. The designs found their way into the tattoos. When Europeans first settled in the islands, they outlawed tattoos, and the practice nearly died out in some places. Today, many of the island people have revived the art of tattooing.

By Design

Traditional Maori tattoos, or *ta moko*, are more than designs drawn on skin. They have meaning special to the person wearing them and are carved into the skin with a special chisel called an *uhi*. Men wore *ta moko* on their face and buttocks, and women wore it on their chin, lips, and shoulders.

Different Strokes for Different Folks

Samoa is one of the few islands where tattooing was kept up even after the arrival of the Europeans. There, the men received the traditional *pe'a*, intricate designs that covered them from mid-torso to the knees. Women got smaller designs on their legs or hands. In Hawaii, tattoos are called *kakau*. They were sometimes meant to guard the wearer's health. Men got tattooed all over, while women got tattoos on their hands, fingers, and sometimes, their tongue.

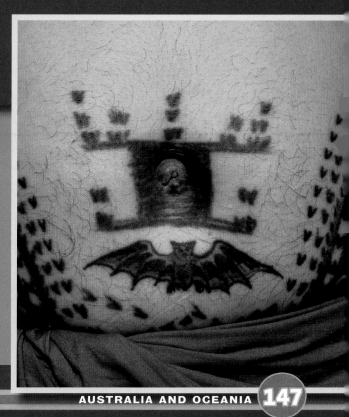

WHERE can you see caves lit by thousands of glowworms?

One day in 1887, a native Maori chief and an Englishman poled a raft into a cave on the North Island of New Zealand. Once their eyes had adjusted to the dark, they saw tiny pinpoints of light reflected in the water. When they looked up, the ceiling of the cave looked like a star-studded sky.

The light came from thousands of tiny glowworms, the larvae of the fungus gnat. Like fireflies, these glowworms use bioluminescence (by-oh-loom-uh-*ness*-ents)— light produced when chemicals in their bodies react to air. Unlike fireflies, they use the light not to attract mates but to lure their favorite food: flying insects.

In caves, glowworms hang silky spiderlike threads up to 18 inches long from the ceiling, each one covered with sticky blobs of mucus. Depending on how big it is, a glowworm can make 15 to 25 lines a night. When the lines are set, the glowworm retreats into a transparent tube of mucus and turns on the lights. When a sticky line snags an insect, the glowworm slithers out of its tube and sucks up the line—and the bug.

Today, the Waitomo Glowworm Caves are one of New Zealand's biggest tourist attractions. Imagine: about 400,000 visitors a year come from far and wide to see the magical light cast by hungry gnat larvae!

Cave Snot

There are even stranger cave creatures than glowworms. Deep inside some caves, certain bacteria thrive where nothing else can live. These bacteria form a slimy film on the walls and ceilings. When the slime on the ceiling gets really thick, it starts to drip. Scientists call these drips snottites. Can you guess why?

All Together Now

North America has its own version of a natural light show. Every year in the beginning of June, thousands of people gather near Elkmont, Tennessee, to watch the fireflies. What makes these fireflies so special? They are one in only 2% of all firefly species to flash at the same time. Usually one firefly starts, and then there's a burst of flashing, sometimes lighting up the whole forest.

WHERE are the Sandwich Islands?

When the English explorer Captain James Cook and his men visited the islands of Hawaii in 1778, he named them the Sandwich Islands after the person who paid for the voyage, the Earl of Sandwich. The name stuck until about 1840, when King Kamehameha III had a constitution drawn up. In it, the kingdom was officially called the Hawaiian Islands.

Even though Hawaii is a U.S. state, it's considered a part of Oceania because it lies way out in the Pacific Ocean. With eight major islands, 10 smaller ones, and more than 100 islets and rocks, Hawaii is the world's longest island chain—and it is still growing.

The Hawaiian Islands started out as volcanoes that formed over a hotspot beneath Earth's crust. Although the hotspot doesn't move, the crust does. As the islands move away from the hotspot, the volcanoes erupt less and less until they stop erupting altogether. Hawaii, or the Big Island, sits on top of the hotspot and has three active volcanoes: Mauna Loa, Kilauea, and Hualalai.

When It Rains, It Pours

Rain falls on Waialeale Peak on the Hawaiian island of Kauai more than 330 days a year. That adds up to 450 inches or more of rain, allowing islanders to claim it's the wettest place on Earth. But two towns in India—Cherrapunji and Mawsynram—claim to get even more rain. Certainly, Mawsynram holds the record for the most rainfall in a single six-month rainy season: about 1,000 inches in 1985!

Running for King

The only U.S. state with a royal palace, Hawaii was ruled by a king before it became a state. When Kamehameha V died in 1872 without naming a successor to the throne, the government held an election. William Charles Lunalilo won but died about a year later. Another election was held and Lunalilo's former opponent, David Kalakaua, became the last Hawaiian king.

CHAPTER 8 Antarctica

Frigid, windy, and dry—that's Antarctica. At 5.3 million square miles, Earth's fifth largest continent is also the southernmost continent. This desolate place is really a desert of ice that's almost 3 miles thick in some areas. In fact, there's so much ice that it makes up 70% of Earth's freshwater supply. Unlike every other continent, there are no permanent human residents in Antarctica. It's a unique natural reserve for scientific research governed by a treaty signed by 50 countries. The Transantarctic Mountains divide the continent into two regions. East Antarctica is the largest, driest, coldest side. West Antarctica includes the Antarctic Peninsula, which is the wettest and warmest part of the continent.

In 1911, Norwegian explorer Roald Amundsen led the first expedition to reach the South Pole.

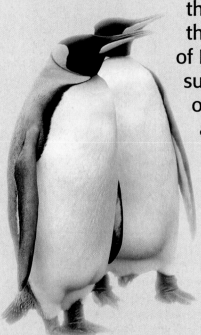

Emperor penguins are the only penguins that live in Antarctica year-round.

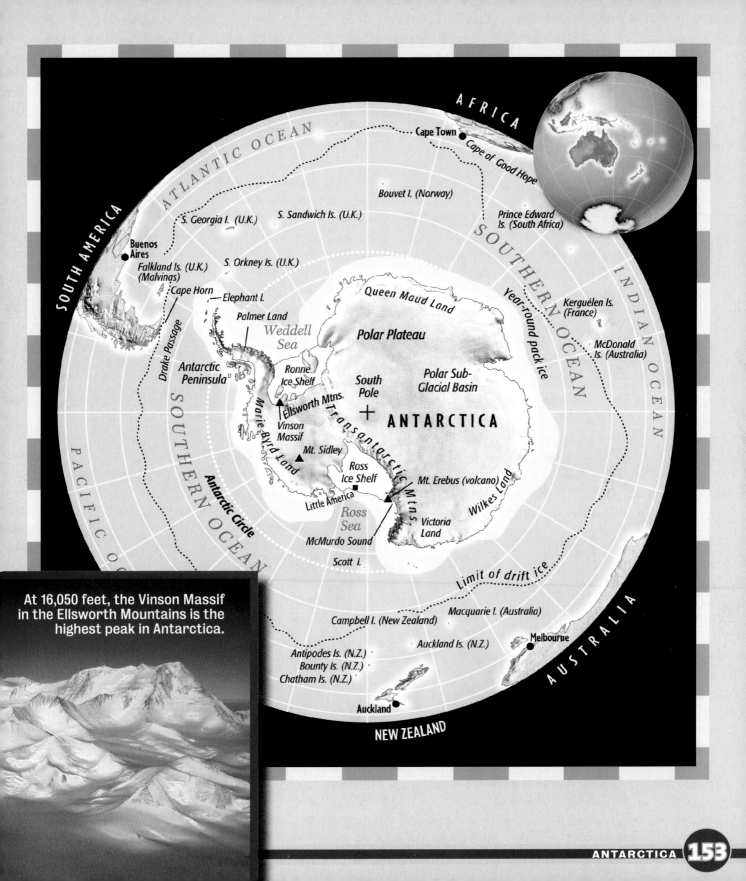

AFRICA

ATLANTIC OCEAN

Cape Town
Cape of Good Hope

Bouvet I. (Norway)

S. Georgia I. (U.K.)   S. Sandwich Is. (U.K.)

Prince Edward
Is. (South Africa)

SOUTHERN OCEAN

SOUTH AMERICA

Buenos
Aires

Falkland Is. (U.K.)   S. Orkney Is. (U.K.)
(Malvinas)

Kerguélen Is.
(France)

INDIAN OCEAN

Cape Horn   Elephant I.

Queen Maud Land

McDonald
Is. (Australia)

Palmer Land

Polar Plateau

Year-round pack ice

Weddell
Sea

Ronne
Ice Shelf

South
Pole

Polar Sub-
Glacial Basin

Antarctic
Peninsula

Drake Passage

Ellsworth Mtns.

Transantarctic Mtns.

ANTARCTICA

Vinson
Massif

Marie Byrd Land

Mt. Sidley

Ross
Ice Shelf

Mt. Erebus (volcano)

Wilkes Land

SOUTHERN OCEAN

Antarctic Circle

Little America

Ross
Sea

Victoria
Land

PACIFIC OC

McMurdo Sound

Scott I.

Limit of drift ice

At 16,050 feet, the Vinson Massif
in the Ellsworth Mountains is the
highest peak in Antarctica.

Campbell I. (New Zealand)

Macquarie I. (Australia)

Melbourne

Auckland Is. (N.Z.)

Antipodes Is. (N.Z.)

AUSTRALIA

Bounty Is. (N.Z.)
Chatham Is. (N.Z.)

Auckland

NEW ZEALAND

WHERE can you find the largest ice-free lake in Antarctica?

About 2.2 miles beneath Antarctica's ice sheet lies the largest lake in Antarctica. Lake Vostok has been untouched by sunlight or weather for about 20 million years. Scientists think it may contain bacteria and other microbes that have survived for all that time in extreme conditions.

In order to get water samples, scientists at Vostok, the Russian research station, had to drill down through the ice. They were close to reaching the lake's surface in early 2012, but they were racing against the weather. The short Antarctic summer was almost over, and temperatures were already down to −45°F. A few degrees colder and it would be too dangerous for aircraft to fly in or out. Just as the scientists were about to stop drilling, lake water shot up into the drilling hole. They had done it! But they had to leave or be stranded.

Several months later, the scientists returned and removed the frozen lake water from the drilling hole. When they tested it, they discovered a new kind of bacteria. Or did they? Some experts think the bacteria came from kerosene used to keep the drilling hole from freezing. Maybe the next sample of lake water will provide the answer.

ice flow

When the ice sheet slides over Lake Vostok, some of the lake water freezes and is carried along with it.

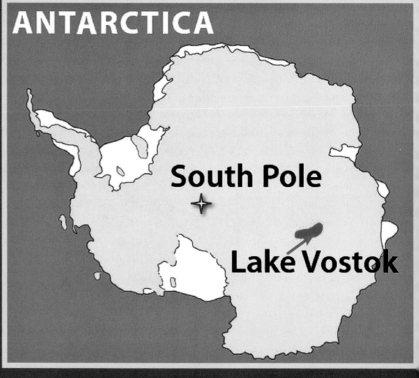

ANTARCTICA

South Pole

Lake Vostok

Summer Cold

Even in December and January, Antarctica's warmest summer months, the average temperature at Vostok is −17°F. One year, it reached a record high of 10°F!

**cored
2.2 miles**

ice sheet

frozen lake water

That's Extreme!

Extremophiles are creatures that survive where it seems impossible that anything could live. They have been found in the Atacama Desert in Chile, in and around superheated seafloor vents, and inside highly acidic rocks in a geyser basin in Yellowstone National Park. It's possible that extremophiles live in Lake Vostok, too.

Life in Space?

Scientists think that liquid water may lie beneath the frozen surface of Saturn's moon Enceladus. If they find signs of life in Lake Vostok, it may indicate that some kind of life could exist on Enceladus, too.

WHERE did an iceberg the size of Connecticut break free?

In March 2000, a huge chunk of ice broke away from the Ross Ice Shelf, a floating sheet of ice attached to Antarctica. The new iceberg was named B-15. With an area of about 4,250 square miles, it was the largest iceberg ever recorded. In May 2000, the iceberg split up.

The largest piece was named B-15A.

Slowly, B-15A drifted west until it bumped up against another iceberg lodged on the eastern side of Ross Island. B-15A remained there until late 2003, when it cracked in two during a storm. The larger part, still called B-15A, shifted

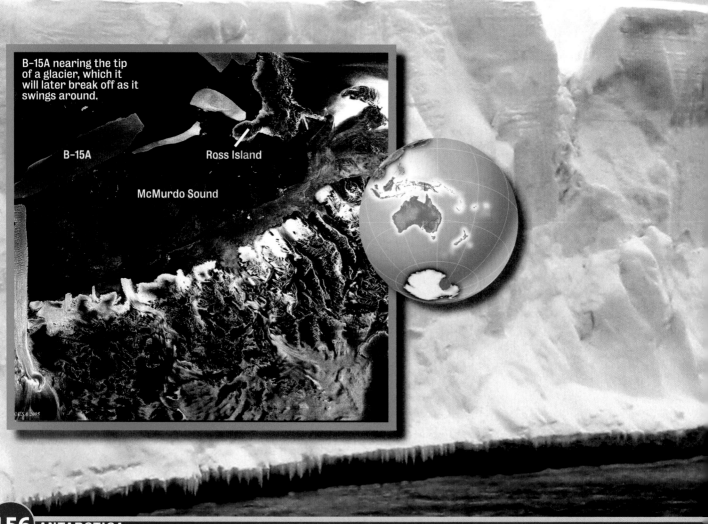

B-15A nearing the tip of a glacier, which it will later break off as it swings around.

B-15A

Ross Island

McMurdo Sound

©ESA 2005

pinnacle iceberg

slightly but continued to block water currents and cause ice to build up in McMurdo Sound for another year. Penguin colonies shrank because adults had to travel much farther to reach their open-ocean hunting grounds. Icebreakers had to struggle to break channels through the ice so supply ships could reach the McMurdo research station, home to U.S. scientists.

In November 2004, B-15A finally started to move again. It knocked off the tip of a glacier and continued along the coast of the Ross Sea. By 2008, the berg had broken up or had melted, disappearing into the sea.

Growlers, Bergy Bits, and Seltzer

Icebergs are floating chunks of freshwater ice that have broken off, or calved, from ice sheets or glaciers. Icebergs come in lots of shapes and sizes. Tabular icebergs, like B-15A, are flat on top and at least five times wider or longer than they are high. Pinnacle icebergs have at least one spire shape sticking up from them. Dry dock icebergs have at least two pinnacles with a deep, U-shaped gap between them. If an iceberg is less than 3 feet above water and 16 feet long, it's called a growler. Bergy bits are icebergs that are 3 to 16 feet above water and 16 to 49 feet long. When icebergs melt, bubbles of ancient air trapped inside are released with a loud sizzling sound—that's called bergy seltzer.

Hot and Cold

Looming over McMurdo Station, a U.S. research center, Mount Erebus is the southernmost active volcano on Earth. An exposed lava lake glows deep inside its crater, and steaming towers of ice dot its snowy sides. The towers are built up as jets of hot gases escape from vents called fumaroles and freeze.

WHERE do mammals live in Antarctica?

Seal lovers have given Antarctica the seal of approval because six species of seals live in the waters and on the ice around the frozen continent. The fiercest are leopard seals, which eat seafood but sometimes prefer to eat penguins and other seals. The biggest seals are bull southern elephant seals, which can grow up to 20 feet long. When challenging other males, the bulls inflate their large noses to make their bellows louder and scarier. Elephant seals are champion divers, going almost 5,000 feet deep and staying under for as long as two hours.

Many whales make their summer home in the waters of the Southern Ocean. Blue whales are not only the largest of the baleen whales but also the largest animals on Earth. How big are they? Adults are nearly 100 feet long and their hearts alone are as big as cars! Among Antarctica's other whales are orcas, the top marine predators better known as killer whales.

leopard seal

Thrills and Krills

Antarctic krill are about the size of your little finger, but their importance is far greater than their size. Millions of these shrimplike sea creatures live in swarms that can spread out for miles and weigh up to two million tons. So what's the big deal? Krill are the main food source of baleen whales and many seals, penguins, fish, and squid.

Fine-Feathered Friends

The most common Antarctic seabirds are penguins. Two of the six Antarctic species—Adélie and emperor penguins—raise their chicks on coastal or sea ice around the continent. The emperor penguin is the largest of the penguins and the only one to breed during Antarctica's frigid winters.

What's Not to Lichen?

Antarctica has no trees or bushes, but it does have about 450 species of plants. Two are flowering plants that grow on the Antarctic Peninsula. The rest are mainly mosses and lichens (*lie*-kenz). There's life even in the harsh climate of the dry valleys, where scientists have found algae growing inside rocks.

It's Not Big, But It's Hardy

At a quarter of an inch long, the wingless midge (a type of fly) is the largest land animal in Antarctica. Larvae can live without oxygen for up to four weeks and survive even if their body fluids freeze.

The Oceans

Oceans cover about three-quarters of Earth's surface. They are both the source of life and important life-support systems. Tiny ocean plants produce more than half the oxygen in the atmosphere, absorb carbon dioxide—which contributes to global warming—and form the base of the food chain. The oceans soak up half the sun's heat and contribute much of the water vapor that rises into the atmosphere and later falls as rain, sleet, and snow.

Pacific Ocean

A blue starfish, or sea star, clings to a coral reef.

More than 90% of all goods transported from country to country are shipped across the oceans.

Arctic
Ocean

Atlantic
Ocean

Indian
Ocean

Southern
Ocean

People enjoy
swimming,
surfing, and
scuba diving in
the ocean.

WHERE is the largest coral reef system?

The Great Barrier Reef stretches 1,242 miles along the east coast of Australia. The reef is so big it can be seen from space. That's pretty amazing, considering that the reef system was built by coral polyps (*pah*-lups), tiny creatures between one-tenth of an inch and 2.2 inches in size. Of course it took millions and millions of polyps thousands of years to build a reef that big.

Corals are related to jellyfish, but the hard corals—the reef-building kind—have stony skeletons that they leave behind when they die. The skeletons form a kind of apartment house for living corals. There are almost 360 species of hard corals in the Great Barrier Reef. Most of them live in large colonies, but each polyp feeds and breeds on its own.

Although hard corals use their stinging tentacles to capture tiny prey, they get most of their food from tiny plants called algae that live inside them. In return for this protection, the algae use a process called photosynthesis to convert sunlight into oxygen and food that provide energy for the algae and the polyp.

A scuba diver follows a potato cod.

A giant clam, which can weigh 400 pounds, spends most of its life in one spot on a coral reef.

Today's Junk, Tomorrow's Reef

People have been building artificial reefs to improve fishing for a long time. That's because reefs offer lots of places for little sea creatures to hide and feed—and for big fish to hang out, waiting for a meal to swim by. Almost anything big and heavy enough can be used to make a reef as long as it's been cleaned up so it won't pollute the water. Some of the things being used today are old ships, subway cars, and tanks.

An artificial reef specially made out of metal

WHERE did the *Titanic* sink?

On the night of April 12, 1912, the *Titanic* was crossing the Atlantic Ocean for the first time. It was about 460 miles southeast of Newfoundland, Canada, when a lookout spotted an iceberg dead ahead. The first officer gave orders to reverse the engines and turn the ship. But it was too late. The *Titanic* sideswiped the iceberg. In less than three hours, the ship broke in two and sank.

At the time, the *Titanic* was the largest, fanciest ocean liner ever built, but it only had 20 lifeboats—enough to hold about 1,200 people. Add to that a skipped lifeboat drill and no general warning that the ship was in trouble, and you have a recipe for disaster. Out of more than 2,200 passengers and crew onboard that night, only about 700 survived.

Lost and Found

The wreck of the *Titanic* lay on the ocean floor for 73 years. Then, in September 1985, searchers sent the *Argo*, an unmanned, remote-controlled submersible, to look for it. Pictures taken by the craft showed the two halves of the ship lying on the ocean floor about 13,000 feet deep—and about 15 miles away from the position given in radio distress signals the night it sank.

Armchair Explorers

In 2012, scientists discovered the wreck of a ship that may have sunk in the Gulf of Mexico 200 years ago. As Internet viewers watched from home via live streaming, underwater robots sent back pictures of the wreck and its cargo. In one photo, a sea anemone (uh-*neh*-muh-nee) seems to be guarding a supply of muskets—old-fashioned front-loading guns.

WHERE is the world's newest island?

On December 19, 2011, Yemeni fishermen saw fiery fountains of lava as high as 90 feet shooting up from the Red Sea. They were not only witnessing a volcanic eruption but the birth of a new island. It surfaced just north of Rugged Island, one of the smaller Zubair Islands off the coast of Yemen. This whole group of islands was created by volcanoes.

About 30 million years ago, magma (thick, superhot melted rock) caused a crack, or rift, in Earth's crust. As the rift widened, the Arabian Peninsula split away from Africa. Water rushed into the rift valley and became the Red Sea. Because the Zubair volcanoes sit on the Red Sea rift line, they are fairly active.

When a volcano erupts underwater, the magma cools quickly into lava. As the lava hardens, it builds up into a mound called a shield volcano. When the mound gets big enough, it breaks the surface of the water and becomes an island.

Hot and Cold

When superhot magma meets cold seawater, it causes explosive volcanic eruptions. These explosions are sometimes called Surtseyan eruptions. The name comes from the birth in 1963 of another island, now called Surtsey, off the south coast of Iceland.

Volcanic eruptions on Surtsey Island

Blown Apart

In 1883, Krakatau volcano on an island in Indonesia exploded, blowing the island apart. The eruption was so loud, people almost 3,000 miles away reported hearing it. But that wasn't the end of the story. By 1930, the volcano had formed a new island called Anak Krakatau (Indonesian for "child of Krakatau"). Since then, the island has grown to about 1,000 feet high and 2 miles across.

Anak Krakatau

WHERE is the hadal zone?

The hadal zone is the name for the deepest parts of the ocean, which are found in steep-sided trenches, or valleys, more than 20,000 feet deep. The very deepest hadal zone is in the Mariana Trench in the South Pacific. It's called the Challenger Deep, and reaches down more than 36,000 feet. The tallest mountain, Mount Everest, could fit inside it with more than a mile to spare.

Trenches form alongside continents and island arcs. Earth's crust is split up into plates (think jigsaw puzzle) that move around on top of the mantle, a layer of superhot melted rock. Ocean plates are heavier than plates carrying land, so when the two crash together, the ocean plate slips under the land plate and forms a deep trench. Most trenches are around the edge of the Pacific Ocean, which is sometimes called the "Ring of Fire" because there is so much volcanic activity.

In ocean trenches, there is no light and the pressure per square inch is eight tons—about the weight of 48 Boeing 747 jets. You wouldn't think anything could live there, but some creatures have adapted to this extreme environment.

Amphipods are little flea-like creatures that have been found as deep as 30,000 feet.

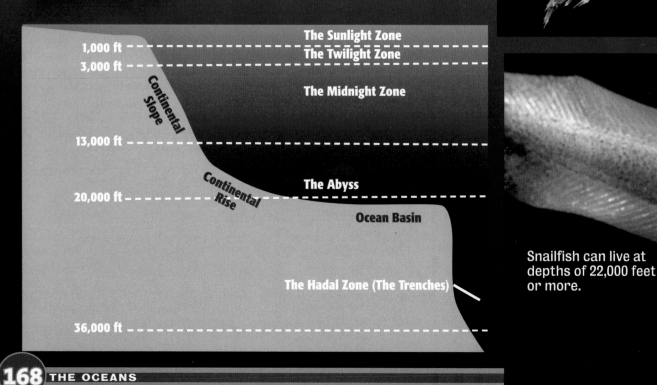

1,000 ft	The Sunlight Zone
3,000 ft	The Twilight Zone
	The Midnight Zone
13,000 ft	
	The Abyss
20,000 ft	Ocean Basin
	The Hadal Zone (The Trenches)
36,000 ft	

Continental Slope

Continental Rise

Snailfish can live at depths of 22,000 feet or more.

Cusk eels have been found as deep as 27,000 feet.

The Longest Mountain Range

The Andes may be the longest mountain range on land, but the mid-ocean ridge system is even longer—by about 35,000 miles! This interconnecting series of underwater mountains stretches all around the world. The ridges are formed where Earth's crust is spreading apart and forming new seafloor. Hot melted rock comes up from the mantle, hits the cold seawater, and erupts, creating new volcanoes at the bottom of the ocean.

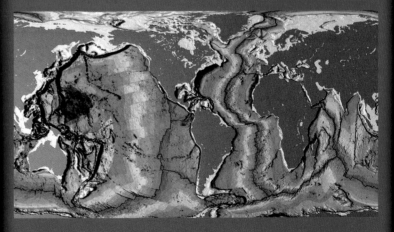

This photo shows undersea mountain ranges. The youngest rock (dark red) is closest to the center of the ridge.

WHERE was the biggest wave ever surfed?

Surf's up! That's a call that really means something in the Atlantic Ocean near Nazaré, Portugal. The area is famous for its huge waves. Several miles wide at the ocean end, a deep underwater canyon narrows as it approaches land—and that funnel shape is what makes big waves even bigger.

That's where American surfer Garrett McNamara caught and rode a 78-foot-high wave in November 2011—and set a new world record for the biggest wave ever surfed. At the same spot on January 28, 2013, McNamara rode another wave that some people say was 100 feet high. But the height will have to be confirmed by experts before his ride is officially declared a new world record.

Hitching a Ride

Surfers don't paddle their boards out to catch giant waves because the waves are too big and too fast. Instead, jet-skis, boats, or even helicopters tow the surfers out to the waves. Once they're at the top of a breaking wave, the surfers let go of the tow-bar—and they're off!

Space

Was there ever life on Mars? Why don't more large asteroids slam into Earth? Where does the solar system end and space begin? Are there other Earth-like planets? These are just a few of the questions that astronomers are answering. Like the crew of the *Enterprise* in *Star Trek* films, these scientists want "to explore strange new worlds, to seek out new life and new civilizations, to boldly go where no one has gone before."

Photos from six spacecraft were combined to make this portrait of the eight planets and Earth's moon.

Spacecraft provide scientists with new information about the sun, planets, asteroids, and comets. This image of Mercury was taken by *Messenger*, the first spacecraft to orbit that planet.

The *Cassini* spacecraft took this picture of Saturn and its rings in 2012.

From 1981 to 2011, space shuttles carried astronauts on missions to repair satellites, do research, and help build the International Space Station. The *Endeavour* made its last trip on October 12, 2012, when it was moved through the streets of Los Angeles to the California Science Center.

WHERE did the Apollo 11 lunar module land on the moon?

On July 20, 1969, the Apollo 11 lunar module touched down on the moon in an area called the Sea of Tranquility. Neil Armstrong, the mission commander, radioed back to Earth saying, "The *Eagle* has landed." Almost four hours later, about 600 million people all over the world watched on TV as Armstrong climbed down and became the first person to set foot on the moon. His words: "That's one small step for (a) man, one giant leap for mankind." Armstrong was soon joined by Edwin "Buzz" Aldrin, the *Eagle*'s pilot.

The two astronauts took photographs, picked up samples of moon rocks, and performed science experiments. They spent a total of 21 hours and 36 minutes on the moon before returning to *Columbia*, the command module, where pilot Michael Collins was waiting. Just over eight days after leaving Earth, the astronauts returned, splashing down in the Pacific Ocean.

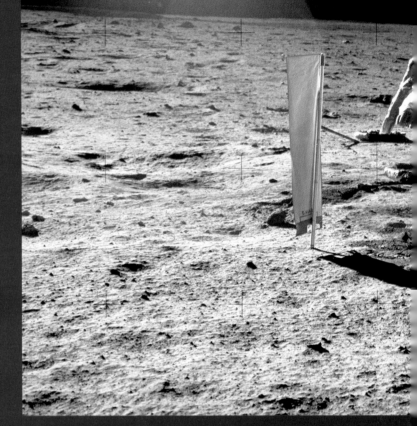

Apollo Program

Six of the Apollo missions landed on different parts of the moon.

July 20, 1969
Apollo 11 landed in Sea of Tranquility

November 19, 1969
Apollo 12 landed in Ocean of Storms

February 5, 1971
Apollo 14 landed in Fra Mauro

Apollo 14 astronaut Alan Shepard on the moon

Neil Armstrong snapped this picture of Buzz Aldrin walking on the moon.

After their return, the Apollo 11 astronauts had to stay away from other people—even their wives—until doctors made sure they hadn't picked up an unknown disease.

Sea of Tranquility

On August 13, 1969, the Apollo 11 astronauts were given a ticker-tape parade in New York City.

July 30, 1971
Apollo 15 landed in Hadley Rille

April 20, 1972
Apollo 16 landed in Descartes

December 11, 1972
Apollo 17 landed in Taurus-Littrow

Technicians check Apollo 17 Mission Commander Eugene Cernan's spacesuit.

WHERE does the solar system end and outer space begin?

We're about to find out. *Voyager 1*, launched in 1977, is on the outer edge of the solar system, about 11.5 billion miles from the sun. The sun's magnetic field is carried into space at high speeds by the solar wind—charged particles given off by the sun. They form a "bubble" called the heliosphere (*hee*-lee-uh-sfeer) that encloses the solar system. In 2004, *Voyager 1* entered the outer reaches of the bubble, where the solar wind suddenly slowed down.

On July 28, 2012, *Voyager 1* entered a new place where the magnetic field of the sun connects to the magnetic field of outer space. Scientists are calling this area the magnetic highway because charged particles from the sun are streaming out while particles from outer space zoom in. They believe it is the last boundary *Voyager 1* has to cross before escaping into outer space.

An artist's illustration of the two *Voyager* spacecraft approaching the edge of the solar system

Voyager 1

Space Twins

Voyager 2 was launched 16 days earlier but it is moving more slowly than *Voyager 1*, its twin. *Voyager 2* has traveled about 9.4 billion miles from the sun. It takes more than 17 hours for radio signals from *Voyager 1* to reach Earth. Both spacecraft will continue sending signals until their nuclear batteries run out. Scientists estimate that could happen in 2020.

Voyager 2

The Golden Record

Both *Voyager* spacecraft carry a message from Earth to any extraterrestrials (aliens) that may find them. The message is on a 12-inch gold-plated copper phonograph record. (The *Voyager* craft were launched five years before the first compact disks were sold and long before digital devices like MP3s and iPods.) The message includes greetings in 55 languages, music, and pictures, as well as instructions on how to play the record using the enclosed phonograph needle.

WHERE in space is an asteroid magnet?

Asteroids are space rocks that can be as small as pebbles or hundreds of miles wide. Many of the asteroids in the solar system orbit the sun between Mars and Jupiter in the asteroid belt. Most astronomers think that these asteroids are leftover rocks that might have become another planet but didn't. And they think Jupiter is the reason why.

Jupiter is the largest planet in the solar system. It's so big that it could hold more than 1,000 Earths. And Jupiter's gravity is strong enough to have kept the rocks in the asteroid belt from pulling together and forming a planet. Astronomers also believe that Jupiter's gravity helps keep the asteroids in their orbit and protects Mars, Earth, Venus, and Mercury from being bombarded by even more space rocks than they already are.

Jupiter's gravity can also act like a magnet when comets and other large space objects careen through the solar system. For example, in 1994, the comet Shoemaker-Levy 9 struck the planet with the energy of 6 trillion tons of TNT.

An artist's illustration of comets approaching Jupiter

Jupiter seen from its moon Europa

Hit and Miss

On February 15, 2013, scientists knew about the big asteroid that would pass between Earth and the moon. What they didn't know was that the 11,000-ton asteroid would hurtle into Earth's atmosphere and explode over Russia in a blinding flash of light. The explosion was equal to about 20 times the energy unleashed by the first atomic bomb. The sonic boom and shock wave shattered hundreds of windows and injured more than 1,000 people.

Shooting Stars

Meteors, or shooting stars, are streaks of light caused by space dust and rocks that burn up when they hit Earth's atmosphere. The dust and rocks are called meteoroids—unless they hit Earth. Then they're called meteorites. When there are more meteors than usual, it's called a meteor shower. These are usually caused by Earth passing through a stream of ice and dust left by a comet.

A meteor shower

WHERE is Curiosity?

Curiosity, a robotic vehicle, or "rover," the size of a small SUV, landed on Mars at 1:25 A.M. on August 6, 2012. Two smaller rovers, *Spirit* and *Opportunity*, had landed on the Red Planet in 2004. The newest and biggest Mars rover touched down in the 96-mile-wide Gale Crater in the planet's southern hemisphere. *Curiosity* is to spend one Martian year (687 Earth days) exploring the crater and climbing the high mountain in its center. It will snap high-resolution pictures with its 17 cameras, and take rock samples to analyze onboard. NASA (National Aeronautics and Space Administration) scientists are hoping to discover whether life ever existed on Mars.

   Curiosity is looking for organics, the carbon-based molecules that are necessary for life to exist. Scientists think they might be found inside rocks. The Gale Crater is a good spot to look because it dates back to about 3.8 billion years ago, when the planet was still covered with water—another requirement for life. *Curiosity* drilled into a rock and tested the powder left by the drill. It showed that life could have existed on Mars—but not whether it actually did.

The Gale Crater on Mars

Searching for Goldilocks

Exoplanets are planets that orbit other stars. So far, scientists have confirmed more than 900 exoplanets and found many more maybes. But what they really hope to find is an exoplanet in the "Goldilocks" zone: just the right distance from its sun so that it won't be too cold or too hot for liquid water to exist. Why? Because that kind of exoplanet may be able to support life as we know it.

Mars Attack!

In October 1938, radio news bulletins warned that Martians had landed in New Jersey and Earth was under attack. Many listeners panicked and hid or got in their cars and tried to flee. It turned out that the "news" was part of a program enacting *War of the Worlds*, a science fiction novel written in 1898. But the actors did such a good job that they made people think the attack was real!

The actor Orson Welles broadcasting *War of the Worlds*

Glossary

algae plants that have no roots, stems, or leaves, and live mainly in water

aquifer an underground layer of porous rock, sand, or gravel that holds groundwater

archaeologist a scientist who studies how people lived in the past

asteroid a space rock that can be tiny or as big as a small planet and orbits the sun; many asteroids are in the asteroid belt between Mars and Jupiter

astronomer a scientist who studies the universe and all that's in it

atmosphere the envelope of gases around Earth

atom the smallest part of an element that can exist by itself or combine with other elements

atomic particle a unit of matter smaller than an atom; also called a subatomic particle

bacteria microscopic single-celled organisms that are found on, in, and around almost everything on Earth

bioluminescence light produced within the body of an animal

boson a class of atomic particles

carat a unit of weight for precious stones and pearls; 1 carat equals .007055 ounce

circuit the complete path of an electric current; also, a group of electronic parts

climate weather conditions in one place over a long period of time

comet a large chunk of rock surrounded by frozen gas and ice that orbits the sun

crystal a substance formed when atoms or molecules are arranged in a repeating pattern

cuneiform an ancient writing system using wedge-shaped characters

decompose the process by which a dead organism rots away

drought a long period of time without rainfall

electron an atomic particle with a negative charge

endangered a word used to describe a species of animal, plant, or fungus that is at risk of becoming extinct

environment surroundings

erode wear away

evaporation the changing of a liquid into a gas or vapor

exoplanet a planet outside our solar system

extinct gone from the world forever

extremophile something that can survive in an extreme environment, such as a superheated seafloor vent

fiber-optic relating to the use of cables enclosing transparent fibers of glass or plastic that transmit light

fjord a narrow, steep-sided inlet of the sea

fossil part of a plant or animal from the distant past that has been preserved in Earth's crust

fossil fuel a type of fuel, such as oil and coal, that is created by plant and animal matter over millions of years

fumarole a hole in a volcanic area that emits hot gases or vapor

fungus a type of organism, including yeast, molds, and mushrooms, that is neither plant nor animal

galaxy a collection of stars and other matter bound together by gravity

generator a machine that changes mechanical energy into electrical energy, often by moving a copper wire through a magnetic field

geothermal energy heat produced inside Earth

glacier a large mass of ice and snow that has been pressed down over thousands of years and which slowly moves forward

global warming an increase in the average temperature of Earth

Gothic style a European style of architecture popular between the 12th and 16th centuries

GPS (Global Positioning System) a satellite navigation system that is used to determine an exact location on Earth

gravity the force of attraction between two objects, which is affected by the size, or mass, of the objects and the distance between them

greenhouse gas a gas, such as carbon dioxide or methane, that helps cause global warming

hadron a type of atomic particle

heliosphere the "bubble" around the solar system that is affected by the solar wind

hieroglyph a type of writing that uses pictures or picture-like symbols to represent words or sounds

humanoid human-like

hydroelectric power electricity produced by harnessing the power of flowing water

iceberg a large floating chunk of ice that has broken off from a glacier or ice sheet

integrated circuit a small chip, usually made of silicon, that can hold up to millions of transistors and other electrical parts; also called a microchip

krill small, shrimplike sea creatures

landfill a site designed to safely bury large amounts of trash

larva the earliest stage (or stages) of an insect, just after it has hatched and before it changes into an adult; the plural is larvae

lava rock that has erupted from a volcano or crack in Earth's surface

lithium the lightest-known metal

magma superhot melted rock beneath Earth's surface

magnetic field the area affected by the pull and push of a magnet or of an object such as the sun or Earth that produces magnetism

mammal a warm-blooded animal that has a backbone and hair or fur, and feeds its young with milk from mammary glands

mantle the layer of Earth beneath the crust

mass the amount of matter in a solid, liquid, or gas

matter anything that has mass and can be measured; the three types of matter are solids, liquids, and gases

Mesopotamia an ancient land that stretched from southern Turkey through Syria and Iraq

meteor a streak of light produced when a space rock burns up in Earth's atmosphere

meteorite a chunk of stone or metal that has fallen to Earth from space

meteoroid a space rock

methane a colorless, odorless gas that burns and can be used as a fuel

microbe a short word for microorganism, a tiny organism such as a bacterium

microchip an integrated circuit

microprocessor an integrated circuit that receives information, performs calculations, and provides results

migration the movement of large numbers of people or animals from one place to another

mucus a thick fluid that coats and protects the nose, throat, lungs, and other areas of the body

nutrient a substance that living organisms need to live and grow

oasis a place in the desert where plants can grow because water is close to or reaches the surface; the plural is oases

orbit the path one body takes around another, such as the path of Earth around the sun

particle a unit of matter or energy, such as an electron, proton, boson, or hadron

pharaoh a king of ancient Egypt

photosynthesis the process by which green plants use sunlight to convert water and carbon dioxide into sugars that give them the energy to grow

pinnacle a tall, narrow structure or high place

plankton tiny organisms that float in the sea and serve as food for fish

plateau a large region of high land that is generally flat

poacher a person who hunts animals illegally

pollutant something that causes pollution

pollution the contamination of air, water, or soil by harmful substances

predator an animal that hunts other animals for food

prehistoric related to a period of time before history was recorded

primate a category of animals that includes humans, apes, monkeys, and lemurs

proton an atomic particle with a positive charge

radio telescope a radio receiver and dish antenna that can detect and use radio waves from space to create detailed images

rain forest a dense forest that grows in regions where it rains heavily throughout the year

ratify to officially approve something

recycle to collect materials, such as metal cans and glass bottles, that have been thrown away in order to reuse them in new products

reservoir an artificial lake that is created by a dam and used to store fresh water

resolution the quality of detail in an image

rift valley a long valley formed when rising magma cracks through Earth's crust

ritual a habit or custom

satellite a natural or manmade object that revolves around a planet

silicon a chemical element often used in electronics

solar wind charged particles given off by the sun

species a group of animals, plants, or fungi that share certain characteristics; members of the same species can interbreed

speed of light 186,282 miles per second

spire the tapered or pointed top of a tall structure

stalactite rock that hangs from the ceiling of a cave like an icicle and is formed by dripping water that contains the mineral calcite

stalagmite rock that rises up from the floor of a cave and is formed by dripping water that contains the mineral calcite; often found under a stalactite

static electricity electricity produced when the positive charges (protons) and negative charges (electrons) in an atom get out of balance

stele (stelae) an upright stone slab or column carved with figures and/or writing; the plural is stelae

strait a narrow waterway between landmasses that connects two large bodies of water

submersible a small craft that can operate underwater

threatened a word used to describe a species of plant, animal, or fungus that is at risk of becoming endangered in the future

tidal bore a surf-like wave formed when an incoming tide forces a river to flow upstream

toxin a poisonous substance produced by plants, animals, and bacteria

transformer a device that changes the voltage of an electric current

transistor the part of a circuit that controls the flow of an electric current

tributary a river or stream that flows into a larger river or lake

tsunami a huge sea wave produced by an earthquake or volcanic eruption

turbine an engine with blades attached to a central shaft; when water, steam, or air flows through the turbine, the blades spin around and produce energy such as electricity

vacuum tube a sealed, mostly airless, glass tube that controls the flow of an electric current

vapor a gas; also tiny but visible particles that float in the air, such as smoke and steam

venom a poisonous substance produced by certain snakes and insects, usually given off in a bite or sting

virus a microbe that can cause different types of illnesses by entering a person's body through the nose, mouth, or breaks in the skin

voltage the force of an electric current

Index

Credits

Continent maps by Joe Lertola. Antarctica and North Pole maps by Joe LeMonnier.

Back cover: Auscape/UIG/Getty Images (background); Tim Graham/Getty Images (tattoo); Leksele/shutterstock (penguins)

2-3: AlenVL/shutterstock (2, top); UIG via Getty Images (2, center); Dale Wilson/Getty Images (2, bottom); Steve Allen/Getty Images (3, top); Atacama Large Millimeter/submillimeter Array (ALMA) (3, bottom left); Caminoel/shutterstock (3, bottom right)

4: Franck Guiziou/Getty Images (top left); Leksele/shutterstock (center right); Maremagnum/Getty Images (center left); Kitch Bain/shutterstock (bottom left); Mulcahey/shutterstock (bottom right)

6-7: Peter Ptschelinzew/Getty Images (6, bottom); ValeStock/shutterstock (6, top); Rafal Cichawa/shutterstock (7, top); Atlaspix/shutterstock (7, center); AlenVL/shutterstock (7, bottom)

8-9: ladywewa/shutterstock (8, left); KingWu/Getty Images (8, right); Jon Schulte/Getty Images (9, top left); Stephen Mulcahey/shutterstock (9, top center); photokup/shutterstock (9, top right); Jose Luis Pelaez Inc/Getty Images (9, bottom left); Leah613/shutterstock (9, bottom right)

10-11: tab62/shutterstock (10, top); Zsolt Biczo/shutterstock (10, center); gielmichal/shutterstock (10, bottom); Tusumaru/shutterstock (11, top left); Serhiy Kobyakov/shutterstock (11, top right); Maartje van Caspel/Getty Images (11, bottom right)

12-13: West Coast Surfer/Getty Images (main photo); UIG via Getty Images (13, top); Andrey Eremin/shutterstock (13, bottom)

14-15: Maurizio Biso/shutterstock (14, left); Thaddeus Robertson/Getty Images (14, top right); tome213/shutterstock (14, bottom right); Michael Bodmann/Getty Images (15, center); National Geographic/Getty Images (15, top right); Paula Bronstein/Getty Images (15, bottom right)

16-17: AFP/Getty Images (16, top); De Agostini/Getty Images (16, bottom left); Stas Volik/shutterstock (16, bottom right)

18-19: Universal Images Group/Getty Images (main image); David Ashby/Getty Images (18); Bernard van Dierendonck/Getty Images (19, top); Georgios Kollidas/shutterstock (19, bottom)

20-21: David Acosta Allely/shutterstock.com (22, top); Universal Images Group/Getty Images (22, bottom); Map by R studio T; British Library/Robana via Getty Images (23, bottom)

22-23: Dale Wilson/Getty Images (main photo); James P. Blair/Getty Images (23, top); Globo via Getty Images (23, bottom)

24-25: John Parrot/Stocktrek Images (main image); Library of Congress (25, top); MPI/Getty Images (25, bottom left); Time & Life Pictures/Getty Images (25, bottom)

26-27: Nataiki/shutterstock (main photo); UIG via Getty Images (27, top and bottom)

28-29: Robert A Isaacs/Getty Images (main photo); David Paul Morris/Getty Images (28); Eros Hoagland/Redux for TIME (29, center); Ann Cecil/Getty Images (29, top right); Michael Davidson/Getty Images (29, bottom left); Bloomberg via Getty Images (29, bottom right)

30-31: Taddeus/shutterstock (30); Creative Commons (31, top); De Agostini/Getty Images (31, bottom)

32-33: Michael Ochs Archives/Getty Images (main photo); GAB Archive/Getty Images (32, left); Redferns/Getty Images (32, bottom); ABC via Getty Images (33, top); Dennis Macdonald/Getty Images (33, museum); Hulton Archive/Getty Images (33, bottom left); Redferns/Getty Images (33, bottom right)

34-35: Hulton Archive/Getty Images (main photo); Library of Congress (35, top); Ernest Sisto/Getty Images (35, bottom)

36-37: Time & Life Pictures/Getty Images (36); Zack Frank/shutterstock (37, top); public domain (37, center and bottom)

38-39: De Agostini/Getty Images (38, top); Manuel Romaris/Getty Images (38, bottom); UIG via Getty Images (39, top); James Randklev/Getty Images (39, bottom)

40-41: Texas Instruments (two main photos); US Army/Getty Images (41, top); Time & Life Pictures/Getty Images (41, bottom)

42-43: Celso Pupo/shutterstock (42, top); Moritz Buchty/shutterstock (42, bottom left); Steve Heap/shutterstock (42, bottom right)

44-45: Atacama Large Millimeter/submillimeter Array (ALMA) (all photos)

46-47: Steve Heap/shutterstock (main photo); Sunshine Pics/shutterstock (46, bottom); Gordon Wiltsie/Getty Images (47, top); DEA/G. Dagli Orti/Getty Images (47, bottom)

48-49: Yolka/shutterstock (48); Mark Van Overmeire/shutterstock (49, top); Jenny Leonard/shutterstock (49, eagle); Andrzej Gibasiewicz/shutterstock (49, bottom)

50-51: AFP/Getty Images (main photo and 51, right); Creative Commons (50, left); Kenneth Garrett/Getty Images (50, bottom); Creative Commons (51, bottom left); public domain (51, bottom right)

52-53: Jacques Descloitres, MODIS Rapid Response Team, NASA/GSFC (main image); Ralf Hettler/Getty Images (52); De Agostini/Getty Images (53)

54-55: Stocktrek Images/Getty Images (main image); Juergen Ritterbach/Getty Images (54, bottom); Steve Allen/Getty Images (55, top); Michael Boyny/Getty Images (55, bottom)

56-57: Dorling Kindersley/Getty Images (56, left); reptiles4all /shutterstock (56, bottom right); Cuson/shutterstock (57, top left); ©2013, University of Illinois Board of Trustees. All rights reserved. Photo by Scott Elrick, courtesy of the Illinois State Geological Survey (57, top right); Bonita R. Cheshier/shutterstock (57, center); Frans Lemmens/Getty Images (57, bottom right)

58-59: Altrendo Images/Getty Images (main photo); AFP/Getty Images (58); Apic/Getty Images (59, top); Hulton Archive/Getty Images (59, bottom)

60-61: All images by Bob Thomas/Popperfoto/Gettty Images except Gamma-Keystone via Getty Images (61, bottom right)

62-63: Sara Winter/Getty Images (main photo); Chris Howey/shutterstock (63, top); Ivan F. Barreto/shutterstock (63, bottom left); Photoshot/Getty Images (63, bottom right)

64-65: Bjorn Holland/Getty Images (main photo); Slow Images/Getty Images (65, top); John Coletti/Getty Images (65, bottom)

66-67: Martin Ruegner/Getty Images (66, top); Mark Harris/Getty Images (Matterhorn); Otto Stadler/Getty Images (69, bottom)

68-69: jirasaki/shutterstock (68, top); Used by permission, © 2012 The LEGO Group (68, bottom); Bloomberg via Getty Images (69, top); isifa/Getty Images (69, bottom)

70-71: Private Collection/Photo © Sphinx Fine Art/The Bridgeman Art Library (main photo); Lonely Planet/Getty Images (71, top); AFP/Getty Images (71, bottom)

72-73: Michele Falzone/Getty Images (main photo); Pavel L Photo and Video/shutterstock (73, top); Caminoel/shutterstock (73, bottom)

74-75: Holger Leue/Getty Images (74); Sebastien Burel/shutterstock (75, top left); Marco Secchi/Getty Images (75, top right); Krzysztof Dydynski/Getty Images (75, bottom left); Joe Petersburger/Getty Images (75, bottom right)

76-77: Bloomberg via Getty Images (main photo); West Coast Surfer/Getty Images (77)

78-79: kan_khampanya/shutterstock (main photo); DEA/G. Dagli Orti/Getty Images (79, Winged Victory); Stuart Dee/Getty Images (79, Mona Lisa); DEA/G. Dagli Orti/Getty Images (79, Hammurabi); National Geographic/Getty Images (79, bottom right); Burlingame Museum of PEZ (79, bottom left)

80-81: Time & Life Pictures/Getty Images (80); Gamma-Rapho via Getty Images (main photo); U.S. Army (81, top); Fotosearch/Stringer/Getty Images (81, bottom)

82-83: Gamma-Rapho via Getty Images (main photo); Illustration by R studio T

84-85: Eisriesenwelt Caves, www.eisriesenwelt.at (84); J. Debru/Getty Images (85, left); VisitBritain/Britain on View/Getty Images (85, right)

86-87: Hung Chung Chih/shutterstock (86, bottom left); SeanPavonePhoto/shutterstock.com (86, top); rujithai/shutterstock (86, bottom right); Zurijeta/shutterstock (87)

88-89: Imagno/Getty Images (88); Map by R studio T; Duncan Walker/Getty Images (89, bottom left); National Geographic/Getty Images (89, bottom right)

90-91: Paul Nevin/Getty Images (90, left); Franck Guiziou/Getty Images (90, right); Huw Jones/Getty Images (91, top); Franck Guiziou/Getty Images (91, center left); David Sutherland/Getty Images (91, center right); AFP/Getty Images (91, bottom)

92-93: Alinari via Getty Images (92); De Agostini/Getty Images (93, top left); Cheryl Forbes/Getty Images (93, top right); UIG via Getty Images (93, bottom left); Fotosearch/Getty Images (93, bottom right)

94-95: AFP/Getty Images (94); Alison Wright/Getty Images (95, main photo); Redferns/Getty Images (95, top right); Gamma-Keystone via Getty Images (95, bottom right)

96-97: EyesWideOpen/Getty Images (main photo); Grant Dixon/Getty Images (97, top); Time & Life Pictures/Getty Images (97, bottom)

98-99: Wei Fang/Getty Images (98, top); Peter Adams/Getty Images (98, bottom); Atul Tater/Getty Images (99)

100-101: Hiroyuki Matsumoto/Getty Images (100); Chad Ehlers/Getty Images (101, left); Chris Mellor/Getty Images (101, right)

102-103: Creative Commons (102, top); Northfoto/shutterstock.com (102, bottom); Map by R studio T; Alexey Avdeev/Getty Images (103, bottom right)

104-105: De Agostini/Getty Images (104, top); Universal Images Group/Getty Images (104, bottom); British Library/Robana via Getty Images (105, top); Peter Dazeley/Getty Images (105, bottom)

106-107: Jane Sweeney/Getty Images (main photo); AFP/Getty Images (106, center); David Fletcher/Getty Images (107, top); Sylvain Cordier/Getty Images (107, center left); Tom Cockrem/Getty Images (107, center right); Rory Gordon and Michael Ramage/Getty Images (107, bottom)

108-109: Attilio Polo's Fieldwork/Getty Images (108, bottom left); njsphotography/shutterstock (108, top); Stu Porter/shutterstock (109)

110-111: Gamma-Rapho via Getty Images (main photo); Sylvain Grandadam/Getty Images (111, top); Ladislav Pavliha/Getty Images (111, sandstorm); Konrad Wothe/Getty Images (111, bottom)

112-113: urosr/shutterstock (main photo); Alistair Duncan/Getty Images (112, bottom); AFP/Getty Images (113, top); Kennet Havgaard/Getty Images (113, sphinx); UIG via Getty Images (113, bottom left); Roberto A Sanchez/Getty Images (113, bottom right)

114-115: Prill/shutterstock (main photo); David W. Hamilton/Getty Images (115, top); Franck Guiziou/Getty Images (115, bottom left); Walter Bibikow/Getty Images (115, bottom right)

116-117: Christian Science Monitor/Getty Images (main photo); National Geographic/Getty Images (117, top left); Gamma-Rapho via Getty Images (117, top right); Maremagnum/Getty Images (117, bottom left); David Wall Photo/Getty Images (117, bottom right)

118-119: Nigel Pavitt/Getty Images (118, bottom); De Agostini/Getty Images (119, top); Sebastien Burel/shutterstock (119, bottom)

120-121: UIG via Getty Images (main photo); Des Bartlett/Getty Images (120, bottom) AP (121, bottom)

122-123: Auscape/UIG via Getty Images (main photo); Hannes Vos/shutterstock (122, bottom); Nigel Pavitt/Getty Images (123, top); Daryl Balfour/Getty Images (123, bottom left); Dave Hamman/Getty Images (plant and beetle)

124-125: Hermann Erber/Getty Images (main photo); Olive/Getty Images (124, bottom); A. & J. Visage/Getty Images (125, top); Danita Delimont/Getty Images (125, bottom)

126-127: Jo Crebbin/shutterstock (main photo); Ann and Steve Toon/Getty Images (127, bottom left); Nigel Pavitt/Getty Images (127, bottom right)

128-129: Hulton Archive/Getty Images (128, top); Anwar Hussein Collection/Getty Images (128, bottom); E. R. Degginger/Getty Images (129, top left); Evans/Getty Images (129, top right); Neal Pratt/shutterstock (129, bottom)

130-131: Fritz Reiss/AP (130, bottom); Mike Derer/AP (131, top left); AFP/Getty Images (131, top right); Bloomberg via Getty Images (131, bottom)

132-133: Brandon Rosenblum/Getty Images (132, left); Eric Isselee/shutterstock (132, right); Nicole Duplaix/Getty Images (133)

134-135: Peter Walton Photography/Getty Images (main photo); Tier Und Naturfotografie J und C Sohns/Getty Images (135, top); Auscape/UIG/Getty Images (135, bottom)

136-137: David Hilcher/shutterstock (main photo); Auscape/UIG/Getty Images (137, top); Kitch Bain/shutterstock (137, bottom left); UIG via Getty Images (137, bottom right)

138-139: Jason Edwards/Getty Images (main photo); Bloomberg via Getty Images (139, top); Tom McHugh/Getty Images (139, bottom)

140-141: Jenny & Tony Enderby/Getty Images (140, bottom); NitiChuysakul Photography/Getty Images (main photo); Robin Bush/Getty Images (141, bottom)

142-143: Tyler Olson/shutterstock (main photo); Michael Runkel/Getty Images (143, top); Tim Laman/Getty Images (143, bottom)

144-145: National Geographic/Getty Images (144); National Geographic/Getty Images (main photo); Paul Chesley (145, top); Mayte Torres/Getty Images (145, bottom)

146-147: Dozier Marc/Getty Images (146, bottom); Patrick Mesner/Getty Images (main photo); Tim Graham/Getty Images (147, top); Peter Hendrie/Getty Images (147, bottom)

148-149: Creative Commons (main photo); Stephen Alvarez/Getty Images (149, top); shay_number823 (149, bottom)

150-151: Dimos/shutterstock (150); Lee Prince/shutterstock (151, left); Luis Castaneda Inc./Getty Images (151, right)

152-153: Leksele/shutterstock (152, left); Universal Images Group/Getty Images (152, top right); Gordon Wiltsie/Getty Images (153, bottom)

154-155: U.S. National Science Foundation (main image); NOAA (155, bottom right)

156-157: Danita Delimont/Getty Images (background); ESA (156, left); Rick Price/Getty Images (157, top); Maria Stenzel/Getty Images (157, bottom)

158-159: Mint Images/Art Wolfe/Getty Images (main photo); 159, from top to bottom: David Tipling/Getty Images; Sylvain Cordier/Getty Images; Eastcott Momatiuk/Getty Images; National Geographic/Getty Images

160-161: Map by R studio T; hxdbzxy/shutterstock (160, left); Ethan Daniels/shutterstock (160, center); homydesign/shutterstock.com (161, right)

162-163: Peter Adams/Getty Images (background); Bob Halstead/Getty Images (162); Len Zell/Getty Images (163, left); Wolfgang Poelzer/Getty Images (163, right)

164-165: Universal Images Group/Getty Images (main photo); Emory Kristof/Getty Images (165, top); NOAA Okeanos Explorer Program (165, bottom)

166-167: NASA (main photo); Ragnar Larusson/Getty Images (167, top); Lund Andersen/Getty Images (167, bottom)

168-169: Diagram by R studio T; Joel Sartore/Getty Images (168, top); Visuals Unlimited, Inc./David Wrobel/Getty Images (168, bottom); National Geographic/Getty Images (169, top); Creative Commons (169, bottom)

170-171: AFP/Getty Images (main photo); Donald Miralle/Getty Images (171, top)

172-173: NASA (172, all photos); NASA (173, top); AP (173, bottom)

174-175: NASA (all photos)

176-177: NASA (176); SSPL via Getty Images (177, top left); Science Source (177, top right); NASA (177, bottom)

178-179: Stocktrek Images/Getty Images (background); Kauko Helavuo/Getty Images (178, bottom); Marat Ahmetvaleev (179, top); Jerry Schad/Getty Images (179, bottom)

180-181: NASA (all photos)

Where are the
highest tides in
the world?

Where was the phrase
"rock and roll" first
used?

Where did the
Titanic sink?

Where is the
Sahel?

Where is the
longest
mountain
range?

Where does the
solar system
end and outer
space begin?

Where did
people first
dance the
tango?

Where can you find the
largest ice-free lake in
Antarctica?